SOCIAL SERVICES
IN BRITAIN

D1665392

LONDON

HER MAJESTY'S STATIONERY OFFICE

1973

Prepared by
REFERENCE DIVISION
CENTRAL OFFICE OF INFORMATION
LONDON

ⓒ *Crown copyright 1973*
First published 1955
Ninth edition 1973

ISBN 0 11 700656 4

N.B. This pamphlet is one of a series produced by the Central Office of Information for British Information Services. To meet requests from inquirers in the United Kingdom, certain pamphlets in the series are being made available on sale from Her Majesty's Stationery Office.

CONTENTS

(*continued overleaf*)

INTRODUCTION

BRITAIN'S social services cover a wide range of provisions to promote the health and well-being of the people and to improve the surroundings in which they live. They have developed with the recognition that the community as a whole has a responsibility both to help its less fortunate members and to secure for all citizens those services which they cannot provide by themselves as individuals.

To give a fuller picture of the provisions that exist to promote social welfare, this pamphlet outlines not only the activities most commonly referred to as 'the social services'—social security, health services, the care of the elderly, the disabled, and children without families, together with education and housing—but also the facilities for promoting good working conditions and helping people to get work, the treatment of offenders against the law, and the provision of legal aid and advice to people without the financial means to defend themselves in court or obtain justice.

Nearly all the services now in being were pioneered by voluntary organisations, especially the churches, and many voluntary services still surround and supplement those publicly and statutorily provided.[1] The two types are not competitive but complementary; public authorities often work through voluntary authorities specially adapted to serve specific needs, and their officials co-operate with the workers of the many social service societies.

The administration of the public services normally takes one of two forms. First, there are services provided directly through central Government departments which make contact with individuals through a network of local offices. Such are the employment and social security services provided by the Department of Employment and the Department of Health and Social Security in Great Britain, and, in Northern Ireland, by the Department of Health and Social Services. (Northern Ireland has its own departments for domestic affairs.) Second, there are services which are administered on a local basis by local authorities but for which the ultimate responsibility rests with central Government departments. These are education, health and personal social services, including child care and housing, which are the concern in England and Wales of the Department of Education and Science, the Department of Health and Social Security, the Home Office, the Department of the Environment and the Welsh Office, in Scotland of the Scottish Office, and in Northern Ireland of the appropriate Northern Ireland departments. In addition, the treatment of adult offenders is a responsibility of the Home Office, Scottish Office and Northern Ireland Department of Home Affairs who are responsible also for the various institutions to which offenders may be sent. In every case ultimate responsibility rests with a minister who is answerable to Parliament, and only Parliament can give authority to undertake any new service.

Although Britain has such a range of services to promote social welfare, it is recognised that the task is never completed. Problems remain to be solved

---

[1] A voluntary society is one which owes its existence to individuals or groups, not to the State, and decides its own policy. A statutory body is one set up by Act of Parliament in order to carry out certain defined functions of government and administration.

and new ones are constantly becoming apparent. Economic conditions can retard or facilitate expansion and the question of priorities must be re-assessed continually; the improvement of services and the very successes achieved in preserving life and raising standards lead to the need for ever-rising expenditure on health, housing, education and other services. Argument and discussion continue as to what are the best ways of organising and financing the services described in this pamphlet, and how they should be adapted to meet the developing needs of the people of Britain.

Moreover, as a member of the European Community, Britain participates in discussing and drawing up social programmes designed to improve living and working conditions throughout the Community.

THE DEVELOPMENT OF THE SOCIAL SERVICES

THE EARLIEST social services in Britain were provided by various religious orders, augmented in medieval times by the manor houses and merchant and craft guilds, which took upon themselves as part of their duties and responsibilities the care of the sick and the destitute. This custom fell into disuse with the decay of the feudal system and the dissolution of the monasteries. By the end of the sixteenth century it had become imperative to find some substitute for the old system. In 1601, therefore, the Poor Law Act was passed, which made it incumbent upon the local authorities in England and Wales to provide from local rates for the sick, the needy and the homeless. A similar Act had been passed in Scotland in 1579. Thus was established the principle that the care of the poor was a necessary part of the social organisation of the State.

The treatment of offenders was recognised as a function of the State comparatively early and became increasingly so, after the Norman Conquest, when the authority of the State became more and more concentrated in the hands of the King. As it was accepted that crimes were committed against the sovereign and the community, punishment came to be based less on the principle of restitution than of providing a deterrent to crime. From Tudor times minor offences were punished with fines, flogging and public humiliation in the stocks or the pillory; more serious crimes were punishable by death (transportation overseas was added as an alternative from the seventeenth century).

The greatest contribution to the social services during the next 200 years came not from the State but from private sources. The eighteenth century, while witnessing a striking evolution in scientific and social outlook, leading to greater humanitarianism in politics, was remarkable more for the achievements of philanthropists and evangelists than for any measures of State-inspired reform.

During the eighteenth century—between 1720 and 1750—11 of London's great voluntary hospitals were founded, as well as 37 in the provinces and 9 in Scotland. In education, the charity schools, established mainly through the Society for Promoting Christian Knowledge, did some excellent work; while the Sunday schools, founded in 1780, began their fight against illiteracy by teaching reading, writing and sometimes 'ciphering'; in preventive medicine, men such as Dr Richard Mead, Dr John Pringle and Dr James Lind succeeded in bringing about much-needed sanitary reforms in the navy, the army, and to a lesser extent in industrial undertakings. The early prison reformers, John Howard and Elizabeth Fry, sought to better conditions in the jails, where prisoners were held awaiting execution or transportation, and William Tuke was experimenting with the care of the mentally ill at The Retreat, York, by gentle methods without the forcible constraint generally applied to the unfortunates locked up in 'madhouses'—when they were not left to fend for themselves or rely on the Poor Law.

The Industrial Revolution and After

The urban and industrial development of the eighteenth and nineteenth centuries exacerbated old problems and created new ones. The Poor Law, progressive in its day, was becoming increasingly inadequate to relieve economic distress. Help was provided by this time mainly through maintenance in the workhouses ('poor houses' in Scotland) where old and young, sick and well, were all mixed together. Only for old soldiers and sailors was there maintenance among their own kind and with some dignity in the two 'hospitals'[1] founded by Royal charity in the seventeenth century or in their own homes by means of 'out-pensions' from the hospital authorities. The workhouses were administered on the principle, enunciated in 1834, of 'less eligibility', that is, that the standard of accommodation and nourishment must be poorer than that of the meanest independent person, so as to discourage wilful idleness. It was not yet appreciated how far unemployment could be due to economic forces beyond an individual's control. The efforts of isolated men and women outraged by the effect of conditions in mines and factories and in the fast-growing industrial towns on the people who lived and worked in them had to overcome both selfish interests and suspicion of State interference before community action to improve matters became possible.

In some matters, notably those connected with industrial health and welfare, the State accepted a measure of responsibility at a comparatively early stage, so that voluntary provision became supplementary, and subject to a certain amount of statutory control. In others, such as education and, later, maternity and child welfare, the State and private organisations continued for years as equal or almost equal partners. The law gave local authorities power to organise and operate services, but it did not compel them to do so; as a general rule voluntary associations were given every encouragement, including grants from the public purse, to carry on their work.

An Act of 1802 marked the beginning of factory legislation, and in 1833 the first substantial Factory Act was passed. This Act limited hours of work for children and set up a national system of inspection. The Act of 1847 set a maximum of ten hours a day on women's as well as children's work; meanwhile the Act of 1844 had introduced the first safety measures. (The scope of all these early Acts was limited to certain factories, mainly textile.) The first Workmen's Compensation Act, making the payment of compensation for accidents at work compulsory and an employer's liability, was passed in 1897.

The early Factory Acts had prescribed for employed children a certain minimum number of hours' education each week. Successive Acts increased this minimum until it was no longer necessary in view of the raising of the age limit below which employment was illegal and the introduction of compulsory education. The State began to take an active part in education in England and Wales in 1870, when the Elementary Education Act provided for the setting-up of schools in areas where the voluntary societies, which had been receiving State grants since 1833, had not already established them. By the end of the century when, in 1899, the Board of Education was created, elementary education had become compulsory, and available free of charge to every child.

---

[1] Chelsea Hospital for old soldiers, Greenwich Hospital for old sailors.

4

Environmental health services were comparatively early recognised as matters for official action. The first true sanitary measure was the Public Health Act of 1848. In the personal health services, on the other hand, voluntary provision remained very important until the establishment of the National Health Service after the second world war. Until then, voluntary hospitals under their own management existed side by side with municipal hospitals under the local authorities, both types making their own distinctive contributions to the welfare of the community as a whole.

In the sphere of housing, State intervention did not begin until 1852 when legislation was passed to permit local authorities to provide lodging-houses for working men and inspect existing ones. The power was permissive only and local authorities were slow to act. The first effective Housing Act authorising local authorities to provide housing at modest rents to supplement that produced by private enterprise was in 1890; it followed weaker measures under which some enterprising authorities had set the example, as in Birmingham's slum clearance drive in the 1870s–1880s which halved the death-rate in the area rebuilt.

Progress towards a gentler and more humane treatment of offenders, particularly young offenders, took place during the nineteenth century. A landmark was the report, published in 1895, of a committee under Herbert, later Lord, Gladstone, which found that although administrative reforms had made prisons more efficiently run and conditions in them more healthy, the punitive regime there did not reform the prisoners but released them brutalised and embittered. The committee recommended that reformation and deterrence should in future be treated as 'primary and concurrent objects'. Its detailed suggestions, including greater differentiation between the needs of the different ages and types of offender, and the initiation while offenders were still in prison of aid to their families and preparation for after-care, were embodied in the Prison Act of 1898.

The late nineteenth century also saw the formation of the National Society for the Prevention of Cruelty to Children and a further growth of small orphanages run by voluntary bodies such as Dr Barnardo's. Conditions in these homes contrasted favourably with those in the large institutions in which the Poor Law authorities cared for orphans, generally unsegregated from other inmates.

An important feature of activity towards the end of the century in which the voluntary organisations led the way was the growth on the one hand of conscious recording and analysis of social conditions,[1] leading to sociological studies and political policies based on systematic observation of facts, and on the other of a more systematic approach to voluntary work for people in distress which fostered better administrative organisation of voluntary bodies and the emergence of social work professions with specialised skills that could be acquired with training.

The Early Part of the Twentieth Century

Even before the first world war, the idea was emerging that social services should not be regarded as a form of charity, but rather as one of the natural

---

[1]For example, Charles Booth's classic survey of London conditions in *Life and Labour of the People* was published in 1889.

benefits available to the citizens of a civilised state, ranking equally with defence, justice, law and order. From these years date the provision of employment exchanges (first opened in 1910) to help workers to find jobs; an old age pension scheme financed from central Government funds, under the 1908 Act, free of the personal indignities of the Poor Law[1]; and an insurance scheme under the National Insurance Act of 1911, providing money payments during sickness or unemployment as of right in return for contributions (limited though it was at first to a small proportion of the employed population). The foundations of the present probation service were laid by the Probation of Offenders Act 1907, which enabled payments to be made from public funds to the voluntary 'court missionaries', and the concept of juvenile courts for young offenders was introduced by the Children Act 1908, which required magistrates to arrange special sessions for the hearing of cases concerned with young people under 16 years.

Stimulated by the experiences of the first world war, which like all wars aggravated existing social problems and created new ones, the State increased its powers and pushed ahead with the development of services to promote health and welfare. During the 1920s and 1930s State support for the maternity and infant welfare services began to make itself felt, through services under the Maternity and Child Welfare Act 1918, which gave local authorities power to provide clinics and similar services. About this period day nurseries and nursery classes were being established for children under the statutory school age, so that children whose mothers were for one reason or another unable to look after them need not suffer from neglect; special schools were being set up for handicapped children, to enable them to make the best of their abilities; the school medical services were being expanded and the provision of free milk and meals in schools was growing so that children whose parents were unable to provide for them in these ways should not be deprived of the medical attention and nourishment necessary to their age. Finally efforts were being made to improve the State elementary and secondary schools, and to provide some sort of further education for young people obliged to leave school at an early age. The Education Act of 1918 raised the upper age of compulsory attendance at school to the end of the term in which the pupil reached his fourteenth birthday; and it charged the local education authorities with the duty of providing advanced instruction and practical training for older children in senior departments or central schools. Also in 1918 came official recognition of the need for youth work,[2] already pioneered by boys' and girls' clubs and other youth movements in the nineteenth century.

Nor was it only the younger generation which benefited from the post-war awareness of the need for the promotion of health and welfare services by the State. Between 1919 and 1939, the State, through the local authorities, assumed additional and specific responsibilities (either directly, or indirectly, by financial help to voluntary bodies) for the care of the blind, the disabled and the

---

[1] The Royal Commission on the Poor Law which reported in 1909 severely criticised the Poor Law system and some of its members recommended its abolition.

[2] State-aided help to young people in starting employment had come earlier when the Education (Choice of Employment) Act 1910 gave local authorities powers to advise young people under 17 on choosing careers.

chronically unfit. Steps were taken to deal more effectively and humanely with socially significant diseases, such as mental disorder or deficiency, tuberculosis, and the venereal diseases. Advances made in curative services such as these were matched by developments in the preventive and general services. The whole question of working conditions in factories came under review, and in 1937 a Factory Act was passed to raise the health, safety and welfare standards. Miners' welfare services were inaugurated on a national scale, while some of the larger commercial companies began to extend their own welfare services and to create new ones; for example, the practice of appointing full-time or part-time doctors and nurses for supervisory duties in factories and workshops began to be much more widely adopted. Between 1919 and 1939, local authorities acquired new powers to provide or promote the provision of housing and a start was made with slum clearance and the alleviation and prevention of overcrowding. The scope and variety of provision for the destitute, outside the Poor Law, rapidly increased. By the outbreak of the second world war in 1939 the social insurance and allied services in Britain comprised: pensions based on need, for the old and the blind (if over 40); unemployment and health insurance and a contributory old-age, widows' and orphans' pension scheme for most manual workers and some non-manual workers; and payments, dependent on need but from central Government funds, to the long unemployed. The war pensions code had been revised in the course of the first world war to provide pensions for the disabled (based on their physical or mental disablement, even if they retained their earning power), and for war widows and orphans, paid by a specially created Government department.

None of these services was imposed by the State upon an unwilling public. All of them were the result of co-operative effort by the successive governments and the people whom they governed. As the new State services were set up, there was no attempt to destroy the spirit of voluntary service which had inspired many of them. Where voluntary organisations were doing good work, they were encouraged to continue, whether it was in school, hospital, or factory, or in the provision of houses. It became the function of the State to supplement the services and provide financial assistance, to see that they were brought within the reach of every citizen, to ensure that adequate standards were maintained, and to hold a balance so that the needs of everyone should, as far as possible, be met.

From the Second World War to the Present
The system of social services which had been achieved by 1939 was good by the standards of its time but it was not comprehensive and there were inadequacies. Like most British institutions, they had grown up at different speeds and with different patterns—the impetus came from some pressing need or some visionary idea rather than a set plan. Then, from 1939 to 1945, for the second time within 30 years, the unsettled and peculiar conditions of war-time focused attention upon the weaknesses and gaps in the existing system. The problems of evacuation showed, for instance, that there were considerable inequalities between some of the medical services provided in the towns and in the country, and that many country districts were still inadequately served. The call-up of young men into the Services showed that,

in spite of progress since the first world war, there was still much to be desired in the standard of their physical fitness and of their intellectual attainments, and that the need to raise the school-leaving age and to provide further education as well as extra opportunities for physical training was an imperative one. The six years' standstill in house-building accompanied by the destructive effect of air bombardment swept away the good effects of the pre-war campaign against the slums and overcrowding, and left behind it a shortage of housing accommodation unequalled after the first world war.

Before the second world war came to an end in 1945, plans were already being made for post-war reconstruction. A series of Acts, beginning in 1944, provided the framework for better and more comprehensive services on which the current provision still rests.

A new Education Act (1944) was passed, raising the school-leaving age to 15 (effective in 1947), with provision for a subsequent advance to 16.

The Family Allowances Act 1945 (effective in 1946), the National Insurance Act 1946 (fully effective in 1948), and the National Insurance (Industrial Injuries) Act 1946 (effective in 1948), were all based on the proposals in the Beveridge Report,[1] published in the middle of the war, which recommended the entire re-shaping of social security provision on a new universal basis.

The provisions of the pre-war legislation on housing and slum clearance were revised by the Housing Act 1949 'to take account of the housing conditions and needs of all members of the community'. The National Health Service Act 1946 and the National Health Service (Scotland) Act 1947 (also effective in 1948) established the machinery for operating a comprehensive National Health Service available to all citizens whatever their means. The New Towns Act 1946, the Town and Country Planning Act 1947, and the Town and Country Planning (Scotland) Act 1947, created the legal framework for rebuilding Britain in a rational and ordered way. The National Assistance Act 1948 removed the last traces of the old Poor Law by providing that anyone in need should be assisted out of central Government funds under a national scheme of assistance, while the Children Act 1948 provided for greater care and a better chance in life for the child deprived of a normal home life. These Acts also took effect in 1948.

The present system of treating offenders in Britain rests largely on the provisions of the Criminal Justice Act 1948 and the Criminal Justice (Scotland) Act 1949, which included provisions abolishing sentences of penal servitude, and hard labour, and embodied the principle that for offenders who could not be dealt with outside prison, for example by probation, the aim of their treatment should be as far as possible reformation and restoration to normal life. In 1949 legislation was passed which widened and reorganised the existing arrangements for free legal assistance to people of limited means.

This series of measures, begun under the wartime coalition Government, was largely based on agreement between all the political parties about the better Britain they wanted to see after the war, and embodied ideas formulated by people of various shades of political opinion. In the planning of the revised and expanded services account was also taken of the findings of a growing volume of specialised social studies undertaken by official and independent bodies.

[1]*Social Insurance and Allied Services*, Cmd 6404, HMSO, 1942.

Since the broad pattern of the current social services was laid down in the 1940s they have not remained static and at present their administration is in the process of rationalisation. The Social Work (Scotland) Act 1968, the Local Authority Social Services Act 1970, the Local Government Act 1972[1] and the National Health Service Reorganisation Act 1973 (together with other similar legislation in Scotland and in Northern Ireland) will result in a complete reorganisation of administrative units and their powers in relation to the provision of social services. In specific fields, the Education Acts 1946 to 1964 clarified and extended certain parts of the 1944 Act and in September 1972 the minimum school-leaving age was raised from 15 to 16. Social security benefits have many times been increased and their scope widened; in 1971 the Family Income Supplement was introduced to help families with small incomes, while between 1970 and 1971 entitlement to pensions was extended to elderly people previously excluded and to widows between the ages of 40 and 50. Other social security benefits were introduced in 1970 and 1971 to help the chronically sick and disabled. Proposals for a new tax credit system (see p 20) have been announced which is designed to integrate the income tax and social security systems and increase the effectiveness of the latter. In the field of employment the Industrial Relations Act 1971 gives an employee protection against unfair dismissal by an employer by enabling him to bring an action and seek compensation. Housing policy, embodied in the Acts of 1961 and 1964, has concentrated on providing increased Government help for house purchase and the improvement of older dwellings. The Rent Act of 1965 provided security of tenure for tenants of rented accommodation and a system of rent regulation, which was extended by the Housing Finance Act 1972, to rented dwellings owned by public housing authorities and housing associations and societies. The treatment of offenders has been greatly reformed. The death penalty was abolished in 1965 and the Criminal Justice Act 1967 introduced the parole system and the suspended sentence among its other changes. The Social Work (Scotland) Act 1968 introduced in Scotland a new system of lay tribunals—child hearings—which deal with children considered to be in need of compulsory measures of care. The Criminal Justice Act 1972 will increase non-custodial methods of treatment and provide for the facilities, such as hostels, which are necessary to service this expansion. Entry to the European Community will result in greater co-ordination over the whole field of social services, for example, the extension of reciprocal arrangements covering health and social security. Closer liaison over educational policy is also planned.

The study of social conditions and research into the causes and prevention of social problems continues and helps to inform public opinion and assist planners. Bodies undertaking or commissioning social research include

---

[1]A reorganisation of local government is planned for England and Wales in April 1974, in Scotland in 1975 and in Northern Ireland in October 1973. Existing authorities in Great Britain will be replaced by county (regional in Scotland) and district authorities. The county or regional authorities will be responsible for major functions such as planning, transport, education and the personal social services, while the district authorities will provide the more local services such as housing and amenities (except in six English conurbations where the district authorities will be responsible for education and the personal social services). In Northern Ireland, local government functions of a regional character are to be transferred to the Northern Ireland departments.

Government departments and the Social Science Research Council, the universities, such voluntary organisations as the National Corporation for the Care of Old People, Age Concern and the National Children's Bureau, and independent trusts, such as the Nuffield Foundation, the National Institute of Economic and Social Research, the National Foundation for Educational Research, the Acton Society Trust and Political and Economic Planning (PEP).

Public Expenditure

The table below showing public expenditure on the principal social services covers expenditure on education in schools, colleges of education, technical institutions and universities; on hospital, general practitioner and local authority health services; on local authority personal social services for the elderly, handicapped and homeless and on child care (figures before 1971–72 relate to welfare services and child care only); on school meals, milk and welfare foods for children and expectant mothers; on national insurance and non-contributory benefits and allowances administered by the Department of Health and Social Security; and on public sector housing, including that in the new towns, subsidies to housing associations, improvement grants and net lending by public authorities for private house purchase and improvement.

UNITED KINGDOM

£ *million*

	1963–64	1967–68	1971–72	1972–73
Education	1,327	2,046	3,163	3,664
National health service ..	1,069	1,588	2,407	2,731
Personal social services ..	85	143	341	412
School meals, milk and welfare foods	103	169	155	166
Social security benefits ..	2,043	3,006	4,578	5,180
Housing	659	1,101	1,292	1,655
Total public expenditure ..	5,286	8,053	11,936	13,808
Current expenditure	4,414	6,646	10,246	11,773
Capital expenditure	872	1,407	1,690	2,035
Total public expenditure ..	5,286	8,053	11,936	13,808
Central government	3,325	4,963	7,590	8,644
Local authorities	1,928	3,010	4,243	5,007
Public corporations	33	80	103	157
Total public expenditure ..	5,286	8,053	11,936	13,808

Source: *Annual Abstract of Statistics*

SOCIAL SECURITY[1]

NATIONAL INSURANCE, industrial injuries insurance, family allowances, family income supplements and supplementary benefits, with (in a special category) war pensions, constitute a comprehensive system of social security.

The Department of Health and Social Security administers these services in Great Britain; within the department the Supplementary Benefits Commission is responsible for the system of supplementary benefits. In Northern Ireland the first five of these schemes are administered by the Department of Health and Social Services which contains the Supplementary Benefits Commission for Northern Ireland. Pensions and welfare services for war pensioners and their dependants are the responsibility of the Department of Health and Social Security throughout Britain. Appeals relating to claims for the various benefits are decided by independent authorities.

Family allowances and national insurance and industrial injuries benefits or allowances, other than maternity, unemployment, sickness, invalidity, injury or disablement benefit, are included in the taxable income on which income tax is assessed. On the other hand, various income tax reliefs and exemptions are allowed on account of age or liability for the support of dependants. Family income supplements, attendance allowance and war disablement pensions are not taxable. Starting in 1972 there are annual reviews of social security benefits. Rates given in the following pages are those in force from October 1973.

Reciprocity

The national insurance, industrial injuries and family allowances schemes of Great Britain and those of Northern Ireland and the Isle of Man operate as a single system. Reciprocal agreements on industrial injuries, family allowances and most national insurance benefits are in operation with Austria, Belgium, Denmark, Finland, the Federal Republic of Germany, Jersey and Guernsey, Norway, Sweden, Switzerland and Yugoslavia. Agreements with Cyprus, France, the Irish Republic, Israel, Italy, Jamaica, Luxembourg, Malta, the Netherlands and Turkey cover industrial injuries and most national insurance benefits. With Australia and New Zealand there are agreements on family allowances and most national insurance benefits. There are limited agreements with Bermuda, Canada and the United States.

The European Community's regulations on social security began to apply to Britain on 1 April 1973. They supersede the existing reciprocal agreements with other Community countries in so far as they apply to nationals of the Community who are employed persons, national insurance pensioners or widows and certain other national insurance beneficiaries and to the dependants of such persons who go to live, work or seek work in another Community country.[1]

FAMILY ALLOWANCES

Family allowances are provided in Great Britain under the Family Allowances Act 1965 (which consolidated the Acts of 1945–64), and in Northern Ireland

[1]For fuller information, see COI reference pamphlet *Social Security in Britain*, R5455.

under its own legislation. They are being paid in Great Britain to over 4·25 million families with over 11 million children, and in Northern Ireland to some 140,000 families. The allowances are payable to families with two or more children who are under minimum school-leaving age or under 19 and either in full-time education or apprentices with low earnings.

The rates of the allowances are £0·90 a week for families with two children below the age limits and a further £1 a week for each additional child.

Family allowances are paid from the Exchequer and their object is to benefit the family as a whole; they belong to the mother, but may be paid either to the mother or to the father. There is no insurance qualification for title to the allowances, but there are certain residence conditions.

FAMILY INCOME SUPPLEMENT

Family Income Supplement is designed to help families (and single people) with small incomes where the wage-earner is in full-time work and there is at least one dependent child. It is payable when the weekly sum of a family's resources falls below a prescribed amount, fixed at £21·50 a week where there is one child plus £2·50 for each additional child. The weekly rate of the supplement is half the difference between the family's income and the prescribed amount up to a maximum of £5 for one- or two-child families or £6 if the family has three or more children. Some 84,000 households containing about 188,000 children and including about 35,000 single people with children are receiving benefit under this scheme.

An identical scheme is in operation in Northern Ireland where some 11,000 households containing about 40,000 children and including almost 1,000 one-parent families are in receipt of the supplement.

NATIONAL INSURANCE

The National Insurance Acts apply, in general, to everyone over minimum school-leaving age living in Great Britain. There are similar schemes in Northern Ireland and the Isle of Man. (The National Insurance Act 1965 consolidated the provisions of the National Insurance Acts 1946–64.)

The national insurance scheme provides benefits in specified contingencies where contribution conditions have been fulfilled. The benefits are paid for partly by insured persons' contributions, partly by contributions of employers in respect of their employees, and partly by a contribution made by the Exchequer out of general taxation.

The original system was based on contributions varying only with the sex, age (under or over 18 years), and insurance class (see below), while benefits were at standard rates for people over 18. Additional earnings-related contributions and benefits were subsequently introduced in two stages (1961 and 1966).

In November 1970 pensions were introduced for elderly people who had been over pension age when the scheme started, and in April 1971 for widows aged between 40 and 50 when widowed or when entitlement to widowed mother's allowance ended. From September 1971 an old person's pension became payable to all other non-pensioners aged 80 and over; at the same time an invalidity pension was introduced for anyone who had received sickness benefit for six months, with an additional invalidity allowance for people where incapacity for work began more than five years before minimum pensionable age. An attendance allowance for severely disabled people needing attendance or supervision both night and day became payable in December 1971. Over the next two years an allowance at a lower rate is being extended to those needing attention or supervision either night or day.

Under Government proposals published in September 1971 and aimed to be introduced in 1975 everyone would have two pensions—a basic pension from the Government and an earnings-related pension from his job.

Contributors

Contributors under the national insurance scheme are divided into three classes:

Class 1. *Employed people.* Most of those who work for an employer under a contract of service or are paid apprentices—over 23 million.

Class 2. *Self-employed people.* Those in business on their own account and others who are working for gain but do not work under the control of an employer—about 1·5 million.

Class 3. *Non-employed people.* All those insured who are not in Class 1 or Class 2—about a quarter of a million.

There is a general liability to pay flat-rate contributions according to this classification but certain people are excepted. These include full-time students, prisoners and most people in receipt of national insurance benefits. Self-employed and non-employed persons whose income is not more than £468 a year can apply for exception. Married women can choose to pay contributions and receive benefit in their own right or not to pay flat-rate contributions (if they are working they must pay graduated contributions) and rely upon their husband's insurance for maternity grant, retirement pension (at a lower rate), widow's benefit and death grant. If a married woman works for an employer he must pay his full share of the flat-rate contributions even if she has chosen not to pay flat-rate contributions.

Flat-rate contributions are credited to full-time students up to the age of 18, and to most people in receipt of national insurance benefits. People who are excepted from liability to pay but are not entitled to credits may pay contributions at the non-employed rate if they wish to safeguard entitlement to retirement pension and widow's benefit.

An employed person ceases to be liable for national insurance contributions at the age of 70 (for a man, 65 for a woman), or when he retires from regular employment after reaching minimum pension age (65 for men, 60 for women), whichever is the earlier. If he does any work as an employed person thereafter, he must pay an industrial injuries contribution; the employer still has to pay his full share of the flat-rate contribution.

Contributions

Flat-rate contributions are normally paid by means of national insurance stamps bought from a post office and fixed, for each contributor, to a single

13

contribution card. All three classes pay flat-rate contributions (see table below). The stamps for Class 1 contributors also include the employer's redundancy contribution (to help to provide for payments in certain circumstances to employees whose work is terminated), and for all contributors the national health service contribution (which for convenience is paid with the national insurance contribution although the two services are separate). It is the employer's responsibility in the first place to see that the Class 1 contributions are paid, but he can deduct the employees' share from their wages. The self-employed and non-employed must stamp their own cards. Flat-rate contributions are usually credited for weeks of unemployment, sickness or injury, or if certain widow's benefits are being paid.

STANDARD ADULT CONTRIBUTIONS*

	Insured Person	Employer	Total
	£	£	£
Employed men:			
Contracted out	0·96	1·247	2·207
Not contracted out	0·84	1·127	1·967
Employed women:			
Contracted out	0·79	1·061	1·851
Not contracted out	0·71	0·981	1·691
Self-employed men	1·93		1·93
Self-employed women	1·61		1·61
Non-employed men	1·52		1·52
Non-employed women..	1·19		1·19

*Including National Insurance, Industrial Injuries and National Health Service Contributions, but excluding Redundancy Fund Contribution. Rates given to three decimal places are expressed in this way for accounting purposes only. Lower rates of contribution are payable for boys and girls and for certain married women.

In general graduated contributions are payable in respect of employed people (including married women) aged between 18 and 70 (65 for women) who earn more than £9 a week. Employees whose job provides them with an occupational pension of at least £3·48 a year for each year of service (£2·90 for women) may be 'contracted out' of part of the graduated pension scheme. Accordingly while all employees pay 5 per cent of their weekly earnings between £18 and £54, contracted out employees pay only 0·75 per cent on their weekly earnings between £9 and £18, while those not contracted out pay the full 5 per cent on this lower range as well. Their employers pay the same amount.

Graduated contributions provide a graduated addition to retirement pension and meet the cost of earnings-related supplements to sickness and unemployment benefit and to widow's allowance. The contributions are collected through the same machinery as is used to collect pay-as-you-earn (deduction at source) income tax and paid into the National Insurance Fund.

14

Benefits

The scheme provides payments to contributors in the event of unemployment (if normally working for an employer), incapacity for work and invalidity (if normally working for an employer or self-employed), and confinement and the weeks immediately before and after (for women normally working for an employer or self-employed and paying national insurance contributions at the full rate). Retirement pensions are paid to people who have reached 65 (60 for women) if they have retired from regular work and from the age of 70 (65 for women) even if they continue to work; people aged 80 and over who have not participated in the scheme are eligible for an old person's pension; widows normally receive benefit in the first 26 weeks after bereavement and subsequently while they have young children or if they have reached the age of 40 when widowed or before their children have grown up; and there are two kinds of allowance in respect of orphan children where a widow's pension is not payable. The scheme also provides lump-sum cash grants for two expensive contingencies—the birth of a child and a death.

For most of the benefits there are two contribution conditions. First, before benefit can be paid at all, a minimum number of contributions must actually have been paid since entry into insurance; secondly, the full rate of benefit cannot be paid unless a specific number of contributions have been paid or credited over a specified period. There are special rules to help a widow who does not become entitled to a widow's pension at widowhood or when her children have grown up, to qualify for sickness or unemployment benefit in the period before she can have established or re-established herself in insurance through her own contributions; there are also provisions to help a divorced woman who was not paying contributions during her marriage.

Amounts

The standard flat-rate benefit for single men and women is £7·35 a week for unemployment or sickness, while for invalidity, widows' and retirement pensions it is £7·75. Benefit, other than invalidity pension for those under retirement pension age, may be reduced if insufficient contributions have been paid, but is not affected by other unearned income or the previous level of earnings. Earnings received while the benefit is in payment, however, may cause its reduction or withdrawal; unemployment benefit cannot be paid to a person earning more than a specified amount from a subsidiary occupation; retirement pensioners under the age of 70 (65 for women) have their pensions reduced in step with earnings over certain specified amounts; sickness and invalidity benefits, though not affected by continued payment of wages during illness, are not normally payable to a person doing any actual work. Widows' benefits, however, are not affected by earnings. Exceptions to the basic flat rates are the higher rate of £10·85 a week payable to widows during the first 26 weeks after bereavement, the increased retirement pension earned by someone who has continued at work and paid contributions beyond minimum pension age and the invalidity allowance paid to people becoming chronically sick more than five years before pension age; and the lower rate of £5·15 a week unemployment or sickness benefit payable to married women who pay contributions and the rates for widows between 40 and 50 which reduce on a scale to £2·33 a week for a woman aged 40 at the date of entitlement. An age addition of £0·25 a week is paid to pensioners aged 80 and over, and people over 80 who have failed to qualify for a national insurance pension receive an old person's pension to bring their total pension up to £4·65 a week (£7·50 for a married couple). Invalidity allowance is £0·50, £1 or £1·60, depending upon the age at which incapacity begins. An attendance allowance of £6·20 a week is paid to severely disabled people requiring a great deal of help from another person both by day and by night. A lower rate of £4·15 may be paid to those who need help either by day or by night.

Additions to benefits are payable for dependants. For invalidity and retirement pensions the additions are £4·75 for a wife or other adult dependant and for these pensioners and for widows receiving widow's benefit £3·80 for each child inclusive of family allowances. For other beneficiaries the additions are less—£4·55 for an adult and £2·30 for each child, inclusive of family allowances.

A guardian's allowance of £3·80 a week is payable to a person who has in his or her family a child who has lost both parents, one of whom was insured under the National Insurance Acts. The allowance can sometimes be paid on the death of one parent. For certain fatherless children there is a child's special allowance also of £3·80 a week inclusive of family allowances; this is payable to a woman whose marriage has been dissolved or annulled and who has not remarried, if her former husband dies and she has a child to whose support he was contributing before he died.

The graduated addition to retirement pension is at the rate of £0·02½ a week for each £7·50 of all graduated contributions paid by a man and for each £9 of such graduated contributions paid by a woman (with, in each case, the matching amount of graduated contribution coming from the employer). The earnings-related supplements to flat-rate unemployment and sickness benefits are one-third of that part of a person's average weekly earnings between £10 and £30 and 15 per cent of that part between £30 and £42, but the supplements cannot raise the total benefit, including increases for dependants, beyond 85 per cent of earnings. The supplement is also paid on this basis to widow beneficiaries who have the appropriate record of earnings, if they become unemployed or sick. A supplement based on the late husband's earnings is also paid, as an addition to the widow's allowance, to widows whose husbands were under 70 and had not retired from regular employment.

A £25 maternity grant is payable for a confinement and a further £25 for each additional child born at the same confinement living 12 hours after birth; while a £30 death grant is payable on the death of an adult (less for a child, or for an adult who was within ten years of minimum pension age when the scheme started).

Duration

In general, national insurance payments are paid as long as the situation requiring them lasts. However, invalidity pension cannot be paid and sickness benefit can only be paid for one year if fewer than 156 contributions have been made (possible in three years for a contributor continuously at work) while unemployment benefit is payable for a maximum of one year. The supplement to unemployment and sickness benefit is paid for a maximum of six months starting from the thirteenth day of unemployment or incapacity for work. Maternity allowance begins 11 weeks before the expected week of confinement and ends after the sixth week following the expected week or the actual week of confinement if this is later.

Similarly, a widowed mother's allowance at the full rate ceases when her children are no longer dependent on her, though a mother can continue to receive £7·75 a week for herself while she has living with her a son or daughter under 19. The widow's pension payable to the childless widow, provided she is 40 or over at the time of being widowed, or the similar pension payable to the widowed mother who has reached 40 before her widowed mother's allowance ends, normally continues until she has reached minimum pension age and retired, or at most till the age of 65. On retirement she receives a pension at a rate not lower than her widow's pension.

INDUSTRIAL INJURIES
The industrial injuries insurance scheme provides benefits for personal injuries caused by accidents arising out of, and in the course of, employment, and for prescribed diseases due to the nature of employment. It covers practically everyone in Class 1 of the national insurance scheme and certain others. Like the national insurance scheme, the industrial injuries scheme is financed partly from contributions and partly from taxation. The legal basis of the scheme is the National Insurance (Industrial Injuries) Act 1965 which consolidated the 1946 Act and subsequent legislation. Similar cover against industrial injuries and diseases is provided by Northern Ireland's legislation.

Benefits
Injury Benefit
Injury benefit for an adult is £10·10 a week plus £4·55 for an adult dependant, £2·30 for the first or only child under the family allowances age limits, £1·40 for the second child and £1·30 for each other child in addition to any family allowance payable. It is paid when the insured person is incapable of work as a result of an industrial accident or prescribed disease, and payment can continue for a maximum of 26 weeks beginning on the date of the accident or development of the disease. A person entitled to sickness benefit who draws injury benefit instead, also receives any earnings-related supplement (see p 16) to which he is entitled.

Disablement Benefit
Disablement benefit may be paid (but not at the same time as injury benefit) when, as the result of industrial accident or prescribed disease, there is a loss of physical or mental faculty. The amount depends on the extent of the disablement as assessed by a medical board; it varies from £12·80 for 100 per cent disablement to £2·56 a week for 20 per cent disablement, but for disablement of less than 20 per cent a gratuity of up to £850 is normally paid.

In certain circumstances disablement benefit may be supplemented as follows: unemployability supplement, at the weekly rate of £7·75; constant attendance allowance of up to £5·15 weekly normally, or a special rate of £7·75 or £10·30 a week in exceptionally severe cases; an allowance of £5·15 a week for exceptionally severe disablement; a special hardship allowance of up to £5·12 for a person who is unfit to return to his regular job or to do work of an equivalent standard; and hospital treatment allowance which raises the benefit to that for a 100 per cent assessment during hospital treatment for the industrial disability. Increases of benefit for dependants are payable with unemployability supplement and hospital treatment allowance. People receiving unemployability supplement may also receive an additional allowance similar to invalidity allowance (see p 15).

Death Benefit

If the accident or disease results in the insured person's death, death benefit may be paid to the dependants.

For a widow a pension of £10·85 a week is payable for the first 26 weeks of widowhood. In addition she receives any earnings-related supplement (see p 16) that would have been paid had she claimed widow's allowance under the main national insurance scheme. Thereafter, the widow can receive a pension of £8·30 a week if she was aged 50 at the date of her husband's death, or has dependent children or other special needs; otherwise she receives £2·33 a week. If she had been living apart from her husband, the pension is limited to the weekly rate of maintenance he was paying, if less than the rate otherwise appropriate.

In addition, allowances are paid for children under the family allowances age limits. For widows, these allowances together with any family allowance payable amount to £3·80 a week for each child. For other beneficiaries, the rate is £2·30 each.

Certain other dependants, such as parents and other relatives, may be entitled to pensions, allowances or gratuities.

SUPPLEMENTARY BENEFITS

The Ministry of Social Security Act 1966 provided for a scheme of supplementary benefits to replace the system which had been administered by the former National Assistance Board since 1948. The Act established within the then Ministry of Social Security a Supplementary Benefits Commission responsible for guiding the scheme and for determining awards of benefit. Parallel legislation in Northern Ireland made similar provision.

Every person in Great Britain aged 16 or over who is not in full-time work, attending school or involved in a trade dispute and whose resources are insufficient to meet his requirements is entitled to a supplementary benefit. The benefit takes the form of a supplementary allowance for people under the statutory retirement age, and a supplementary pension for those over. The benefit is the amount by which a person's requirements exceed his available resources, both being defined by rules laid down by the Act. The calculation of requirements is based on different amounts for single people and family groups (for blind people there are special higher amounts) with, in each case, an addition for rent. For the old and most other long-term cases a special addition is made. Available resources include certain income and capital; the main national insurance and industrial injury benefits, family allowances, family income supplement and maintenance payments from a husband or the father of the claimant's children are taken into account in full but some part of all other resources is disregarded.

The payment of a supplementary allowance in the case of an able-bodied person of working age may be conditional on registering at an employment exchange of the Department of Employment. The allowance is then paid at the exchange; otherwise it is paid weekly through a post office.

The Supplementary Benefits Commission also has a duty to influence people without a settled way of living to lead a more normal life. The commission provides temporary accommodation for them in 19 reception centres, three of which are administered by local authorities on behalf of the commission (see p 37). For men who have been unemployed for long periods and who are receiving supplementary allowances or are using reception centres, it runs 14 re-establishment centres, three of which have residential accommodation, where they are given help to fit them again for work. The commission also makes grants towards the running costs of establishments which are similar to reception or establishment centres and run by voluntary organisations.

WAR PENSIONS AND RELATED SERVICES

Pensions and allowances for people disabled or bereaved through war or service in the Forces since the second world war are paid under Royal Warrants and other instruments administered by the Department of Health and Social Security.

The basic pension for 100 per cent disablement for a private soldier is £12·80 a week, but the amount varies according to rank and the degree of disablement. The latter is assessed by comparing the condition of the person disabled by service with that of a normal healthy person of the same age and sex. Allowances for a wife and children are paid in addition to the basic pension. There is a wide range of supplementary allowances, the main ones being for unemployability (£8·40 a week), constant attendance (up to £5·15 and, exceptionally, £10·30 a week), comforts (£1·10 or £2·20 a week), and lowered standard of occupation (up to £5·12 a week). An age allowance (between £0·60 and £1·80 a week) is payable to disablement pensioners who are aged 65 or over and whose assessment is 40 per cent or more.

Both the basic disablement pension and the supplementary allowances are free of income tax, and children's allowances are paid in addition to any family allowances payable.

Pensions are also paid to war widows and war orphans. The standard rate of pension for widows of private soldiers is £10·10 a week, with additional allowances for their children and, in certain cases, a rent allowance (up to £3·90 a week). There is an additional allowance for widows aged 65 which is increased at age 70. Parents or other relatives who were dependent on a person whose death resulted from service in the Forces may receive pensions if they are in financial need.

The Department of Health and Social Security maintains a welfare service for war pensioners and war orphans which is available to help any who require advice or assistance. War pensioners have priority for treatment of their war disablements in National Health Service hospitals subject only to needs of emergency and other urgent cases.

Many voluntary associations and ex-Service organisations give financial aid and personal service to disabled ex-Service men and women and their families.

The department's welfare officers work in close co-operation with these and other statutory bodies.

THE TAX-CREDIT SYSTEM

In October 1972 the Government presented to Parliament proposals for a tax-credit system which, if approved, would take some five years to bring into operation. The scheme is designed to eliminate a degree of avoidable overlap between income tax and social security and to replace the PAYE income tax system with something easier to operate and understand.

The main feature of the tax-credit system, which would cover about 90 per cent of the population, is that the main personal tax allowances would be replaced by tax credits on family circumstances. Credits would normally be set against tax payable on earnings or on the main national insurance benefits, but where the credit was greater than the tax the difference would be paid as an addition to the wage or other income. Child tax allowances and family allowances would be replaced by child credits.

The national insurance scheme would continue as would the supplementary benefit scheme. But the number of people who would need to draw supplementary benefit would be substantially reduced. In almost all cases the tax-credit system would provide a greater measure of family support than family income supplement, which would be discontinued except for a few people outside the scheme. If the scheme were approved it would provide a substantial and comprehensive benefit to lower-paid workers and to a large number of pensioners. It would identify need more efficiently and less intrusively and relate benefit to it more accurately, eliminate many of the present anomalies and obviate the problem of people not claiming the benefits to which they are entitled.

HEALTH SERVICES[1]

SERVICES concerned with public health together with the personal health provisions of the National Health Service are described in this chapter; measures to promote the health and welfare of employees at their place of work and of school children are described in the sections of this pamphlet on employment and education.

PUBLIC HEALTH

The Public Health Acts of 1936 and 1961 and the Health Services and Public Health Act 1968 constitute the present basic public health code in England and Wales. Local authorities (under the general direction of the Department of Health and Social Security or the Welsh Office and the Department of the Environment) have extensive powers for making and administering by-laws on matters of public health. The local authorities chiefly concerned are the councils of counties and county boroughs, London boroughs and the City of London, borough, urban and rural district councils and, to a limited extent, parish councils.

Public health services in Scotland and in Northern Ireland have developed on much the same lines as in England and Wales, although they are based on separate Acts and there is a different allocation of services between the various types of local authority (working under the direction of the Scottish Home and Health Department and in Northern Ireland the Department of Health and Social Services and the Department of Development). The Public Health (Scotland) Act 1897 and the Burgh Police (Scotland) Act 1892 as amended by later statutes constitute the basic legislation for Scotland. The local authorities concerned are the councils of counties and burghs. In Northern Ireland the councils of county and non-county boroughs and urban and rural districts are mainly responsible for administering the Public Health Acts (Northern Ireland) 1878–1971. Some responsibility for the provision of public health services in Britain will pass from local authorities to the new area health boards to be created under the reorganisation of the National Health Service. Public health aspects of environmental health will, however, still remain a local authority function. In Northern Ireland responsibility for water and sewerage services are to be transferred to the Department of Development.

Control of Infectious Diseases

The medical officers of health of local authorities are responsible for investigating outbreaks of infectious diseases and for disinfection and various other preventive measures. Port health authorities exercise health control at seaports and airports, to prevent the introduction of infectious disease and the entry of unfit or otherwise unsound foodstuffs. Control is undertaken by health authorities using the service of medical officers, public health inspectors, rodent inspectors and others.

---

[1]For fuller information, see COI reference pamphlet *Health Services in Britain*, R5154.

Pure Food

The purity, hygiene and description of food are controlled by the Food and Drugs Act 1955 in England and Wales, by the Food and Drugs (Scotland) Act 1956 in Scotland and by the Food and Drugs Act (Northern Ireland) 1958 in Northern Ireland.

In England and Wales the composition, adulteration and description of food are the concern of food and drugs authorities (county, county borough, London borough and City of London councils and, generally, the larger borough and urban district councils), while its soundness, purity and hygiene are the concern of all local authorities, except parish councils. The Department of Health and Social Security and the Ministry of Agriculture, Fisheries and Food are the central departments responsible for giving advice and making regulations. Places where food for sale for human consumption is prepared, sold or stored must conform to certain hygienic standards. Authorised officers of the councils may take for analysis or for bacteriological or other examination samples of any food for sale for human consumption. Special regulations are in force for certain foods such as milk, meat and ice-cream.

In Scotland the local authorities chiefly concerned are the councils of counties and large burghs. In Northern Ireland administration is in the hands of the county and county borough health committees, the central department being the Department of Health and Social Services.

Other Public Health Duties

Local authorities are also responsible for the public health aspects of water supply, sewerage and drainage; street paving and housing; and the abatement of noise nuisance. They have power to establish smoke-controlled areas to secure cleaner air, and to arrange with statutory water undertakings for the addition of fluoride to water supplies to reduce dental decay.

THE NATIONAL HEALTH SERVICE

The Acts setting up the National Health Service—the National Health Service Act 1946, the National Health Service (Scotland) Act 1947 and the Health Services Act (Northern Ireland) 1948—came into force simultaneously on 5 July 1948.

The object of the National Health Service Act 1946 was 'to promote the establishment in England and Wales of a comprehensive health service designed to secure improvement in the physical and mental health of the people of England and Wales and the prevention, diagnosis and treatment of illness, and for that purpose to provide or secure the effective provision of services'. The service is available to people normally resident according to medical need, without regard to any insurance qualification. It was originally free to users but various charges have been introduced under subsequent legislation, though these can be waived under certain conditions.

National insurance contributors are required to pay a weekly national health contribution but contributors and non-contributors are entitled to the same full range of services. Visitors from other countries who come to Britain specifically for treatment are expected to pay for it, but treatment can be given under the emergency provisions of the National Health Service to any who fall ill or meet with an accident during a visit to Britain. Reciprocal health agreements have been concluded between Britain and certain countries.

The health rules governing Britain's membership of the European Community took effect from 1 April 1973. Under these rules British nationals who are employed persons or receiving national insurance or industrial injuries benefits are entitled, together with their dependants, to medical treatment in another Community country when visiting or living or working there. This treatment is provided under the legislation of the country involved and in some of them persons receiving treatment have to pay part of the cost.

Health Service Administration in Great Britain

The general form of the organisation established in 1948 to administer the National Health Service has persisted ever since. Essentially it has been a tripartite structure, corresponding to the three main parts of the service: the hospital service, the general practitioner service and the local health authority services, comprising a range of home and clinic services for prevention of ill-health and for treatment or care. A new and functionally unified National Health Service administration for England and Wales on a country and area basis is to come into operation from April 1974 under the National Health Service Reorganisation Act 1973 at the same time as the new structure of local government. Under the National Health Services (Scotland) Act 1972, Scottish health services will be reorganised on an area basis from April 1974 too, though this will be earlier than the reorganisation of local government in Scotland, which is due to take place in 1975.

In the meantime the National Health Service in Great Britain continues to be organised as follows:

1. The hospital and specialist services for which the Secretary of State for Social Services, the Secretary of State for Wales, and the Secretary of State for Scotland are directly responsible. These are administered by 20 regional hospital boards and some 400 hospital management committees, or, in the case of teaching hospitals, boards of governors or, in Scotland, boards of management.

2. The family practitioner services which consist of the family doctor service, the dental service, the pharmaceutical service and the ophthalmic service. They are administered by 157 local executive councils on which doctors, dentists, pharmacists, ophthalmic medical practitioners and opticians are represented. The health ministers have indirect overall responsibility for the services.

3. The local authority health services.

In addition, the Secretary of State for Social Services and the Secretaries of State for Wales and Scotland have power to conduct, or assist others to conduct, research work and they provide a public health laboratory service and a blood transfusion service. The Secretary of State for Social Services and the Secretary of State for Wales are advised by the Central Health Services Council, by standing advisory committees on various aspects of the service and by the Hospital Advisory Service, set up in 1969, on hospital problems, in particular those of 'long stay' hospitals. The Secretary of State for Scotland is similarly assisted by the Scottish Health Services Council and its committees.

Medical and dental schools are not under the control of the health ministers in England and Wales but it is their responsibility to provide hospital clinical facilities for the training of medical students. The universities are responsible for the provision of teaching.

The Secretary of State for Scotland has similar duties.

The Northern Ireland Health Services are described separately on p 31.

Proposed Reorganisation

The central feature of the proposed administrative reorganisation of the National Health Service for England, Wales and Scotland will be the establishment of area health authorities (health boards in Scotland) responsible for all health services in their area, including the community health services and the school health service. These area authorities will in general cover the same areas as the new major local authorities but will be quite independent of them, though they will co-operate on many matters. Within the areas there will be districts, each with a district general hospital serving a population usually of not more than 250,000 people, though there may be some considerably larger districts. In Scotland and Wales the area authorities will report directly to the Scottish and Welsh Offices respectively, but in England, because of its greater size, there will be an intermediate tier of regional authorities between the area authorities and the Department of Health and Social Security.

The authorities, both area and regional, will consist mainly of unpaid part-time members, appointed in the case of regional authorities by the health minister concerned (the Secretary of State for Social Services), but in the case of area authorities also by local authorities and universities.

Public representation in the reorganised service for England and Wales is to be provided by district community health councils. These will consist of 20–30 members, half of them appointed by local government district councils and the rest mainly on the nomination of voluntary bodies.

In Scotland local health councils will be set up by the health boards to represent the interests of the public and report on questions relating to the health service in their area or district. The Parliamentary Commissioner for Administration (Ombudsman) has also been designated as Health Service Commissioner to deal with complaints from the public in England and Wales and in Scotland.

Finance

Expenditure on the health and personal social services in Britain was estimated at £2,933 million in 1972–73. The greater part of the cost falls on the Exchequer and is met from general taxation, and a part is met from local rates. Other income is derived from the national health service contribution paid with the national insurance contribution and from charges paid by people using certain services.

There are charges for prescriptions (except for children under 15, women who are expecting a child or who have had one in the past 12 months, people aged 65 and over, patients suffering from certain medical conditions, war and

Service pensioners, and families in receipt of supplementary benefits and family income supplement); for treatment in the dental service (but not for examination only or for treatment given to people under 21 years or to women who are expecting a child or who have had one in the past 12 months); for dentures (except for children under 16 or still at school, and women who are expecting a child or who have had one in the past 12 months); for spectacles (except children's standard spectacles); and for certain other articles and for some local authority services (see p 28). Certain exemptions or refunds are made on income grounds. A limited number of beds may be made available for hospital patients wishing for privacy, provided that this accommodation is not needed on medical grounds for non-paying patients; a charge for part of the cost of the accommodation is made. Provision is also made at certain hospitals for patients to be treated as private patients on payment of the whole cost of their accommodation and treatment. Such patients may make private arrangements for treatment by doctors of their own choice.

Hospital medical staffs are either full-time and salaried, or part-time; part-time medical officers are usually paid on a sessional basis and are free to accept private patients. General medical practitioners in the National Health Service are paid according to the amount of work and responsibility they undertake; certain practice expenses are also directly reimbursed.

Dentists providing treatment in their own surgeries are paid on a prescribed scale of fees according to the treatment they have carried out. Pharmacists dispensing on their own premises are paid on the basis of the prescriptions they dispense. Ophthalmic medical practitioners and ophthalmic opticians taking part in the general ophthalmic service are paid approved fees for each sight test made; opticians who dispense spectacles are paid according to the number and type of pairs supplied.

GENERAL PRACTITIONER SERVICES

The general practitioner services cover the medical attention given to individuals by doctors and dentists of their own choice from among those taking part in the service. Doctors and dentists normally work at their own surgeries; practice in health centres established under the National Health Service Acts is increasing. About 98 per cent of the 25,000 general medical practitioners (principals and assistants) in Great Britain take some part in the service, more than 75 per cent of them in partnership or group practice. The attachment of local authority midwives, health visitors and home nurses to doctors' practices is becoming more widespread.

Doctors wishing to enter practice have to apply through the executive council for the area to the Medical Practices Committee, so that a balanced distribution of doctors throughout the country may be facilitated. The maximum number of patients' names permitted to be on a family doctor's list is normally 3,500; the average number in Great Britain is about 2,400. It is normally through the patient's own doctor that access to most other parts of the health service is obtained.

There are about 11,000 dentists in England and Wales and some 1,000 in Scotland in the general dental service.

Some 900 ophthalmic medical practitioners and over 6,000 ophthalmic and dispensing opticians in England and Wales, and about 70 ophthalmic medical practitioners and about 650 ophthalmic and dispensing opticians in Scotland are engaged in the general ophthalmic services. These services provide for the testing of sight and provision of spectacles. Patients requiring treatment are dealt with through the hospital eye service.

There are about 11,900 retail pharmacies under contract to the National Health Service in Great Britain. They are responsible for the dispensing of all prescriptions except for the small number dispensed by certain general practitioners and hospital pharmacies.

HOSPITAL AND SPECIALIST SERVICES

The hospital and specialist services provide hospital accommodation of all kinds, including district general hospitals with treatment and diagnostic facilities for in-patients, day-patients and out-patients, hospital maternity departments, infectious disease units, psychiatric and geriatric facilities, rehabilitation facilities, convalescent homes and all forms of specialised treatment.

Hospitals

A large proportion of the hospitals in the National Health Service were built in the nineteenth century; some trace their origins to much earlier charitable foundations, such as the famous St Thomas' and St Bartholomew's hospitals in London. Much has been done in recent years to improve and extend existing hospitals, some of which are housed in inconvenient buildings, and a number of new hospitals have been built. In 1962 long-term plans for hospital building were published by the Government, and a revision made in 1966 set out the probable future pattern of the hospital service and contained assessments of the work to be undertaken in the ten years ahead. These plans were revised upwards in 1972, and it is intended to spend £800 million on hospital building in England in 1971–72 to 1975–76 compared with £550 million in the previous five years.

Of the hospitals in the National Health Service some 2,500 are in England and Wales, including the 25 teaching hospitals in London (actually groups of hospitals, convalescent homes, branches, annexes and treatment centres, numbering over 100 altogether) and the 10 teaching hospitals elsewhere in England and Wales (comprising some 50 hospitals and other establishments). They have 450,000 beds available for use and a nursing and midwifery staff of nearly 207,000 full-time and about 116,000 part-time. There are 360 hospitals in Scotland with 65,000 beds and over 31,000 full-time and over 17,000 part-time nurses and midwives.

A small number of hospitals remain outside the service for special reasons. Most of these are run by religious orders. Some, such as the Italian and Jewish hospitals, were set up to serve a special group of patients; others are maintained for the chronic sick or for convalescents by charitable organisations. There are also private nursing homes which must be registered.

Rehabilitation

Rehabilitation is an important aspect of medical care and today treatment is not limited to the relief of pain or cure of pathological conditions but aims at helping people to resume normal living as soon as possible. Medical rehabilitation has been applied with advantage in the care of many patients, including the chronic sick, the mentally disabled, the aged and the handicapped and has enabled many patients to become self-sufficient and to resume an independent life in their own homes. Specialised medical rehabilitation facilities are provided in the majority of hospitals and at medical rehabilitation centres. The work is carried out under the supervision of the appropriate medical specialist by physiotherapists, remedial gymnasts, occupational therapists and social workers acting as a team. The hospital departments work closely with the Disablement Resettlement Service of the Department of Employment. Reports published in 1972 by sub-committees of the Standing Medical Advisory Committees of the Central and Scottish Health Services Councils called for improved co-ordination and development of medical rehabilitation services.

Medical rehabilitation includes the provision, free of charge, of artificial limbs and eyes, hearing aids, surgical supports, invalid chairs, certain types of invalid vehicles, and other appliances. Nursing aids for the handicapped at home can be borrowed through the service.

Social workers are available in most hospitals to help those patients who have difficulties connected with their illness. They help to solve social and emotional problems and are concerned with the rehabilitation and resettlement of patients especially where the illness has been long or where the disability results in changes in the patient's life. From April 1974 social work in hospitals will become the responsibility of the local authority social service departments.

Drug Dependence

The hospital service plays a major part in the treatment of drug dependence, providing treatment for both in-patients and out-patients either in specialised drug dependence units or as part of the general psychiatric service. Only doctors licensed for the purpose by the Home Secretary may prescribe heroin and cocaine to addicts in the treatment of addiction and all medical practitioners are required to notify the Chief Medical Officer of the Home Office of any person they consider to be addicted to dangerous drugs.

Abortion

The Abortion Act 1967, which came into force in Great Britain in 1968, permits the termination of a pregnancy by a registered medical practitioner if two registered medical practitioners are of the opinion that its continuance would involve risk to the life of the pregnant woman, or of injury to the physical or mental health of the pregnant woman or of any children in her family greater than if the pregnancy were terminated, or if there is a substantial risk that if a child were born it would be seriously physically or mentally handicapped. An abortion may be carried out in National Health Service hospitals or in premises approved for the purpose by the Secretary of State concerned.

Blood Transfusion

The National Blood Transfusion Service in England and Wales is administered by the regional hospital boards under the National Health Service. Donors give their blood voluntarily without payment. There are two central laboratories administered by the Medical Research Council on behalf of the Department of Health and Social Security: the Blood Group Reference Laboratory, which prepares grouping serum and investigates blood grouping problems referred to it, and the Blood Products Laboratory, which prepares dried plasma and plasma fractions. In Scotland the Blood Transfusion Service is under the direction of the Scottish National Blood Transfusion Association, which is an independent voluntary body but is supported in the main by a grant from the Scottish Home and Health Department. In Northern Ireland the Blood Transfusion Service is operated by the Northern Ireland Hospitals Authority.

Chest Radiological Service

A Chest Radiological Service, which is freely available, is provided by chest clinics and the radiological departments of general hospitals. The success of mass radiography units has been such that their work is being phased into the hospital radiography service. Mobile X-ray units are still used among especially susceptible groups.

Bacteriological and Virological Laboratory Services

The Public Health Laboratory Service provides a network of bacteriological and virological laboratories throughout England and Wales which conduct research and assist in the diagnosis, prevention and control of epidemic diseases. Its largest establishment is the Central Public Health Laboratory at Colindale, in north-west London, which includes the National Collection of Type Cultures, the Food Hygiene Laboratory, and reference laboratories specialising in the identification of infective micro-organisms.

In Scotland there is no separate public health laboratory service and bacteriological work is done mainly in hospital laboratories. In Northern Ireland a central public health laboratory shares the bacteriological work with hospital laboratories.

Safety of Medicines

Under the Medicines Act 1968 the health and agriculture ministers of Britain are responsible for licensing the marketing, manufacture and distribution of medicines for human and veterinary use. The Medicines Commission has been established as an advisory body to the ministers on policy regarding medicines. The statutory Committee on the Safety of Medicines set up by the commission assesses the safety, efficacy and quality of medicines for human use while the Veterinary Products Committee advises on veterinary products.

LOCAL HEALTH SERVICES

The major local authorities—in England and Wales counties, county boroughs, London boroughs and the City of London and in Scotland counties and large burghs—are health authorities and, as such, provide through their health departments a number of health services under the National Health Service, including maternity and child health services, family planning, domiciliary midwifery, home visiting, vaccination and immunisation, the prevention of illness and the care and aftercare of people who are ill. With a few exceptions, these services are without charge to their users.

To ensure that these services bring the maximum help to those who use them, local health departments work in close co-operation with the general practitioner and hospital and specialist branches of the National Health Service, and with the social service departments of their own local authorities.

As a result of the proposed reorganisation of the National Health Service (see p 24) area health authorities will assume responsibility for all health services in their areas which will in general cover the same areas as the new major local authorities.

Care of Mothers and Young Children

Services for mothers and young children involve the provision of preventive health services, including dental care for expectant and nursing mothers and for children under the age of five years. All local health authorities provide maternity and child health clinics. They are usually staffed by full-time local authority medical officers, or by general practitioners employed on a sessional basis and by health visitors. An increasing number of family doctors are undertaking this work for their own patients in their surgeries, in health centres (see p 31) or in maternity and child health centres. An important function of the child health clinic is routine medical examination and assessment of the child's developmental progress to detect early signs of mental, emotional and physical defects so that prompt treatment can be instigated to prevent or mitigate the development of a condition that might cause handicap. Parents can visit child health centres whenever they feel in need of advice from the doctor or the health visitor; otherwise arrangements can be made for the health visitor to call on a child at home.

Under the welfare foods scheme, a pint a day of free milk and free vitamins are available to expectant mothers in families in receipt of supplementary benefit or family income supplement or in special need because of low income and to every child under five in such families. Milk is also available irrespective of income to expectant mothers who are already bringing up two children under five; all families bringing up more than two children under five in respect of the third and subsequent such children; and to all handicapped children aged 5–16 who are not registered pupils at a school or special school. Children attending an approved nursery or playgroup or with an approved child-minder are entitled to one-third of a pint free on each day of attendance.

For those not entitled to a free supply, national dried milk, children's vitamin A, B and C drops and Vitamin A, D and C tablets for expectant and nursing mothers are available at economic prices from child health clinics and other welfare food distribution centres.

Domiciliary Midwifery Service

All local health authorities have a duty to ensure that adequate numbers of midwives are available in their area to attend women having their babies at home. The expectant mother may arrange to have her baby in hospital or at home according to the advice given by the doctor or midwife. Some 85 per cent of confinements in England and Wales and 96 per cent in Scotland take place in hospital. For a home confinement the services of a general practitioner obstetrician who may be her own family doctor besides those of a trained midwife are available to every mother. The midwife takes part in the care and health education during the antenatal period and cares for mothers and babies (whether born at home or in hospital) in their own homes for ten days after the birth. After this health visitors visit the home to give advice to parents on the care and development of babies and on health education in general. Most premature babies are cared for in hospital but special arrangements for those who are fit to remain in, or return to, their own homes are made by many local health authorities who lend equipment and appoint experienced nursing staff to supervise their care.

Family Planning

Under the National Health Service (Family Planning) Act 1967, local health authorities are able to provide advice on contraception and contraceptive supplies for any person who seeks them. This service may be provided either directly by the authority, or through the agency of a voluntary body such as the Family Planning Association. Local health authorities are also empowered, through the National Health Service (Family Planning) Amendment Act 1972, to include vasectomy within the range of their family planning services. Domiciliary family planning services are becoming more widely available. No charges are made where drugs or appliances are supplied on medical grounds but they may be made in non-medical cases depending on the means of the recipient. An increasing number of local authorities are providing an entirely free family planning service.

When the National Health Service is reorganised in April 1974 the new area health authorities will be obliged to provide services which will include advice on family planning and prescriptions for supplies.

Health Visiting

It is the duty of local health authorities to provide, in their areas, the services of health visitors to visit persons in their homes to give advice on the care of young children and to expectant and nursing mothers, to persons suffering from illness and to elderly people. Increasingly their work is in close association with general medical practitioners as members of primary health care teams and they maintain frequent liaison with the hospital service.

Home Nursing

Nurses are employed by local health authorities or sometimes by voluntary organisations acting on behalf of those authorities, to attend people who require nursing in their own homes, in health centres or elsewhere. The training lasts 16 weeks for state registered nurses and 10 weeks for state enrolled nurses. The service has greatly expanded during the last few years, partly because of the earlier discharge of patients from hospitals and partly because of the increasing number of old people in the community.

Vaccination and Immunisation

All local health authorities make arrangements for vaccination against diphtheria, measles, poliomyelitis, rubella, tetanus and whooping cough at local health authority clinics or by family doctors. Vaccination against tuberculosis is arranged by local health authorities through the School Health Service and chest clinics.

Prevention of Illness, Care and After-care

Local health authorities have power, subject to the Secretary of State's approval, to make arrangements for the prevention of illnesses, such as tuberculosis, or the care or after-care of persons who are or have been ill.

Other services provided by all or almost all local authorities include chiropody; the supply or loan of nursing equipment; and arrangements for recuperative holidays. Many authorities make arrangements for taking cervical smears for pre-symptomatic screening for cervical cancer. Authorities may also make arrangements for the adaptation of patients' homes to accommodate dialysing equipment provided by hospital authorities.

A charge may be made for some of these services if the person wishing to make use of them can reasonably be expected to contribute towards their cost.

Health Centres

There has been a marked increase of interest in health centres at which facilities can be made available for the provision of medical, dental and pharmaceutical services and consultant and other hospital out-patient services in association with local authority services. In July 1973, 459 were in operation in England and Wales, 203 were under construction and many more planned. In Scotland, where the provision of health centres is primarily the responsibility of the Secretary of State for Scotland, there were 47 centres in operation, 19 under construction and many more planned.

Ambulance Services

Free conveyance by ambulance in England and Wales between home and hospital is provided, where needed, by local authorities either directly or by arrangement with voluntary organisations. The Hospital Car Service (organised by the St John Ambulance Association and Brigade, the British Red Cross Society, and the Women's Royal Voluntary Service) augments the ambulance service in many areas by the conveyance of sitting patients. In Scotland ambulances are run by the St Andrew's Scottish Ambulance Service on behalf of the Secretary of State for Scotland. In Northern Ireland they are run by the Northern Ireland Hospitals Authority.

HEALTH AND WELFARE SERVICES IN NORTHERN IRELAND

The health services established under the Health Services Acts (Northern Ireland) correspond fairly closely to the system under the National Health Service in Great Britain and are financed in the same way as in the rest of Britain. Personal social services are provided under the Welfare Services (Northern Ireland) Act 1971 by separate statutory welfare authorities.

The hospital and specialist services, which include mental health services, are administered on behalf of the Department of Health and Social Services by the Northern Ireland Hospitals Authority through hospital management committees. The Northern Ireland Hospitals Authority has under its control 98 hospitals containing in all about 18,000 beds. The administration of the general medical, dental, pharmaceutical and general eye services is in the hands of the Northern Ireland General Health Services Board, which takes the place of the executive councils in Great Britain. There are some 751 general practitioners (with an average of 2,095 patients each), 335 dentists, 12 ophthalmic medical practitioners and 127 ophthalmic and 9 dispensing opticians. The provision of health centres is the responsibility of the Department of Health and Social Services. The range of local authority services are similar to those already described for the rest of Britain.

Plans are in hand to replace the existing tripartite arrangement for the provision of health and personal social services by a unified structure in which these services will be provided by four Health and Social Service Boards acting as agents of the Department of Health and Social Services. The services to be integrated include hospital and specialist services, local authority health and welfare services, and general health services. The transition to the new structure will be synchronised with the reorganisation of local government and it is intended that the area boards will assume their functions in October 1973.

PRIVATE MEDICAL TREATMENT

Though practically all residents in Britain use the National Health Service, a number of people sometimes prefer to pay for private consultations and treatment. Among the major users are the families of the million or so subscribers to the provident schemes which make provision for private health care in return for annual subscriptions (now about £24 million or 2 per cent of the expenditure on NHS hospital and specialist services).

HEALTH EDUCATION

Health education in England, Wales and Northern Ireland is the responsibility of the Health Education Council which assists in the development of programmes of health education with local authorities, professional organisations, voluntary bodies and industry. There are separate arrangements in Scotland. Expenditure is met largely from central Government funds.

MEDICAL RESEARCH

Government funds for medical research in Britain are channelled through the University Grants Committee whose general grants to universities cover research as well as teaching; the Medical Research Council (see below); and the Health Departments which support research in aid of the National Health Service in universities, hospitals, other Government departments and industry. Further support is provided by a large number of charitable foundations and organisations, such as the Cancer Research Campaign and the

Nuffield Foundation; and there is substantial investment in medical research and development by the pharmaceutical and medical equipment industries.

Medical Research Council

The Medical Research Council supports work both in its own establishments—which include the National Institute for Medical Research, the Laboratory of Molecular Biology and the Clinical Research Centre, and in over 70 research units—and by means of research grants for projects in university and other centres. The programme includes fundamental studies of the structure and natural processes of the body; clinical and laboratory studies of disease; the development and evaluation of special methods of treatment and also of prophylaxis and diagnosis; the study of social and occupational factors affecting health and the efficiency of body and mind; and the development of methodology and tools for research.

The council is assisted by three advisory boards which cover its main fields of work—the Clinical Research Board, the Biological Research Board and the Tropical Medicine Research Board—and by a number of scientific committees concerned with specific research problems.

PERSONAL SOCIAL SERVICES

IN ENGLAND AND WALES, the Local Authority Social Services Act 1970, which came into operation in 1971, integrated the administration of personal social services by the responsible local authorities by allocating the relevant functions, previously undertaken by several committees, to a statutory social services committee. In this reorganisation, the Act was carrying out the principal recommendations of the Seebohm committee.[1] The services in question are those provided for the social well-being of the elderly, the disabled, the mentally disordered, the physically handicapped, the homeless, young children, and deprived or delinquent children (see also section on child care p 38). Similar arrangements were introduced, under the Social Work (Scotland) Act 1968, in Scotland, where local authority social work committees under directors of social work are additionally responsible for the duties undertaken by the probation service in England and Wales (see p 89).

The responsible local authorities in England and Wales are the councils of counties and county boroughs, the London boroughs and the City of London and in Scotland of counties and large burghs. District councils in England and Wales are, however, also empowered to provide meals and recreation for the elderly.

The ministers centrally responsible for the personal social services are the Secretary of State for Social Services in England and the Secretaries of State for Wales and for Scotland. In England and Wales the ministers will be advised on matters relating to the personal social services by a new Personal Social Services Council.

THE ELDERLY[2]

A number of services are provided by statutory and voluntary bodies to help elderly people to live in their own homes for as long as possible. The services which local authorities are empowered to provide—in addition to health services (see p 28)—include domestic help, sitters-in, night attendants and laundry and meals services as well as day care, clubs, recreational workshops and transport to get there. Social workers employed by local authorities and voluntary organisations are spending an increasing proportion of their time helping old people and their families with their problems—in many areas in close collaboration with 'good neighbour' and friendly visiting services arranged by the local authority or a voluntary organisation.

Local authorities also provide residential accommodation for the elderly and infirm and have powers to register and inspect homes run by voluntary organisations or privately. The newer homes provided by local authorities for elderly and other infirm people vary in size according to local needs but usually have accommodation for 30 to 50 residents. About 2,400 homes for elderly people are provided by local authorities in England and Wales which house about 2 per cent of the population over 65.

[1]The committee's recommendations were published in 1968 in the *Report of the Committee on Local Authority and Allied Personal Social Services*, Cmnd 3703, HMSO.
[2]For fuller information, see COI reference pamphlet *Care of the Elderly in Britain*, R5858.

Elderly people enter homes only when it is clear that they need more help than can adequately be provided in other ways. The care provided is intended to be of the kind a person might expect to receive in his own home. Rules are kept to a minimum and the residents are free to come and go as they choose, and to receive visitors. In addition to care and attention, board, lodging and laundry, etc, the various amenities provided may include chiropody, hairdressing, newspapers and periodicals, radio and television, entertainments, outings and holidays. Residents are assessed to contribute towards maintenance according to their means subject to the payment of a minimum weekly charge prescribed by the Secretary of State and to the retention of a prescribed weekly sum for personal requirements. The aggregate of these two prescribed sums is equal to the amount of the basic social security retirement pension. Where necessary, the Supplementary Benefits Commission (see p 18) will make a grant to bring a resident's resources up to this amount.

In addition to residential accommodation, local authorities have, under the Housing Acts, provided an increasing number of smaller dwellings for old people, and flatlets for frail or infirm old people who can lead independent lives with some help (see p 75). Local authorities may contribute towards the cost of employing a warden to undertake welfare duties in such specially designed housing.

THE DISABLED[1]

Included under this heading are the mentally disordered and the physically handicapped.

The Mentally Disordered

Local authorities have a duty to make arrangements for helping the mentally disordered in the community, and for prevention and after-care services. Recent developments in the treatment of mental illness, which enable patients to be discharged from hospital more quickly provided support is available in the community, are adding to the demands for these services. Arrangements include training centres for the mentally handicapped, day care and occupation centres for the mentally ill, as well as social centres and residential accommodation for the mentally disordered of all ages. Local authorities are expected to keep in touch with officers of the Department of Employment so that the mentally disordered may be encouraged to progress to sheltered or open employment; and to assist in the rehabilitation of the mentally ill.

In Scotland, education authorities share the responsibility for providing training or occupation and in England and Wales responsibility for mentally handicapped children is with the education departments.

The Physically Handicapped

Local authorities have a duty to provide social services for people who are blind, partially sighted, deaf, hard of hearing, or otherwise substantially or permanently handicapped.

---

[1]For fuller information, see COI reference pamphlet *Rehabilitation and Care of the Disabled in Britain*, R4972.

The chief causes of handicap are arthritis and rheumatism, organic nervous diseases, and injuries. The majority of handicapped people are elderly, but there are many of all ages, including some with congenital conditions. Thus the number of people provided with residential accommodation by local authorities in England in March 1972 was 113,500 of whom 102,900 were over 65. The Survey of the Handicapped and Impaired carried out by the Office of Population Censuses and Surveys and published in 1971 estimated that, of the handicapped at home needing support, 65 per cent were over 65.

Local authorities are required to secure full information on the number of handicapped people in their area and on their needs. A wide range of facilities with which voluntary organisations give important help is available, including advice on occupational, social and personal problems arising from disability; assistance in overcoming the effects of disability; help in carrying out adaptations in the home—for example, by fitting ramps, widening doorways, installing ground floor lavatories, guide rails, and providing various aids to living to meet individual needs, including, in certain circumstances, a telephone; specially designed housing; the means of access to public buildings; social and occupational centres and clubs; teaching of handicrafts and other occupations either at home or in centres; and the provision of recreational facilities, outings and holidays. They also provide residential homes for the severely handicapped. In particular, local authorities are encouraged to give special attention to providing separate accommodation for younger physically handicapped people—that is, those between the ages of 17 and 50. Their needs are different from those of elderly handicapped people who have come into care late in life and who can usually live suitably in ordinary homes for the elderly where they have the companionship of their contemporaries. The aim is to provide for the younger physically handicapped an environment in which they can lead as active, independent and varied a life as their disabilities allow.

Help available for handicapped people from other sources includes financial aid, preventive and medical treatment, special education, training for employment and placement.

THE HOMELESS

The National Assistance Act 1948 required local authorities to provide temporary accommodation for persons in urgent and unforeseeable need and for other persons as determined by the authority. This was intended primarily to meet emergencies such as fire or flood, though eviction was always envisaged as a possible reason for temporary accommodation. In fact with the continuing housing shortage the main use of this accommodation has become the provision of a roof for families who have no housing accommodation, and some temporary accommodation has come to be provided under the Children and Young Persons Act 1963 as an alternative to taking children into care. At the beginning of 1973, 4,395 families (20,370 people) were in temporary accommodation in England. Increasingly local authorities are also providing social work support, rent guarantees, and other services aimed at preventing homelessness and rehabilitating families with difficulties.

In addition to the provisions made by local authorities, the Supplementary Benefits Commission (see p 18) maintains 16 reception centres in various parts of the country for people 'without a settled way of life' and a further three are run by local authorities on the commission's behalf. These centres provide accommodation for 2,500 people, who are homeless, destitute and unsettled. Their purpose is to provide a skilled assessment so that those coming to a centre may be dealt with according to their need for medical and social services, or simply for accommodation. The centres try to encourage the men and women who go there to settle down. Where appropriate and possible, they are referred to specialist services, such as those for the mentally ill. Those who stay receive any necessary medical treatment from visiting doctors and are helped to regain the habit of work and to find lodgings outside.

Voluntary organisations like the Salvation Army and the Church Army provide accommodation, in particular, for homeless single people, in their hostels and lodging houses. In addition groups such as Christian Action, Shelter, the Cyrenians and the Simon Community Trust have done much valuable work in finding accommodation for homeless people. At present the Supplementary Benefits Commission is grant-aiding 21 voluntary projects which provide accommodation and services analogous to the commission's reception centres.

Hostels also exist for the care and rehabilitation of special groups such as alcoholics and ex-offenders. There are rehabilitation hostels in England and Wales.

DAY CARE OF CHILDREN

Day care services are provided for those children with special needs or whose mothers have no option but to go to work and for those who for special health or social reasons need day care.

Apart from nursery schools and playgroups, there are in Great Britain about 460 day nurseries with places for some 25,000 children under five. They are provided by local authorities and voluntary organisations. Private nurseries and playgroups which provide for approximately 200,000 children must be registered with the local authority to ensure that their premises and management are satisfactory. People who mind children (other than relatives) under five years of age in their homes for payment must also be registered. The authorities have powers of inspection and supervision in respect of these registrations and powers to impose requirements regarding, for example, standards of care and accommodation.

CHILD CARE AND ADOPTION[1]

CHILD CARE

Included in the range of personal social services of local authorities in Britain is the duty of care and protection towards children who have no parent or guardian willing and able to provide for them and control them adequately. Local authorities in England and Wales are empowered under the Children and Young Persons Act 1963 to make available such advice, guidance and assistance as may promote the welfare of children by diminishing the need to receive or keep them in the authority's care or to bring them before a juvenile court. This help may include assistance in kind, or, exceptionally, financial help, and may be given through a voluntary organisation or directly. Alternatively, under the Children and Young Persons Act 1969 a child may be committed to the care of a local authority under a care order if the juvenile court, having considered all the child's circumstances, is satisfied that he is in need of care or control which he would be unlikely to receive unless the court made an order. In England and Wales local authorities have a further duty, under the Children Act 1948, to receive into their care any child under the age of 17 who has no parent or guardian, or who has been abandoned or whose parents are unable to provide for him temporarily or permanently. If the child is committed to care by a court he remains in care until he is 18 years old. Otherwise, it is the duty of the local authority to return him to his parents as soon as it is appropriate. The parents of a child in care under the 1948 Act can remove their child at any time, unless the authority has passed a resolution to assume parental rights. Both those children received into care and those committed are treated so as to further their best interests and afford them opportunity for their proper development. In Scotland, under the provisions of the Social Work (Scotland) Act 1968, the juvenile courts were replaced by a system of children's hearings which have powers to impose compulsory measures of care on a child by means of a supervision requirement which can remain in force until he is 18 years old.

When practicable, children in care are boarded out with foster parents, who get an allowance to cover maintenance. If a child cannot be found a foster home, or is not suitable for boarding out, he may be placed in residential accommodation usually provided by a local authority or a voluntary organisation or cared for in any other manner appropriate to his case. The Children and Young Persons Act 1969 provides for regional planning of accommodation for children in care of local authorities by the provision of community homes. These homes comprise local authority children's homes and a range of voluntary homes which become 'assisted' or 'controlled' together with approved schools and remand homes (see p 42) which will gradually cease to function as such. In Scotland local authorities are responsible for providing appropriate accommodation for children in their care. The desirability of returning a child to his family circle as soon as possible is fully appreciated, and work is carried out to rehabilitate the family where this is necessary.

In England and Wales local authority child care functions are the responsibility of the social services committees appointed under the Local

[1]For fuller information, see COI reference pamphlet *Children in Britain*, R5236.

Authority Social Services Act 1970. In Scotland child care work is undertaken by local authority social work departments set up under the Social Work (Scotland) Act 1968. Regulations for England and Wales for children in care of local authorities and voluntary organisations and the conduct of children's homes are made by the Secretary of State for Social Services and the Secretary of State for Wales and, for Scotland, by the Secretary of State for Scotland.

In Northern Ireland the welfare authorities of each county and county borough (under the general direction of the Department of Home Affairs) are responsible for caring for homeless and neglected children under the Children and Young Persons Act (Northern Ireland) 1968. Arrangements for child care follow the same general principles as in Great Britain.

Voluntary organisations, many of which were pioneers in child care, continue to play a valuable part in this work. The larger societies, such as Dr Barnardo's, the Church of England Children's Society and the Catholic Child Welfare Council are constituent societies of the National Council of Voluntary Child Care Organisations, to which a large number of smaller voluntary homes are also affiliated. In Scotland a valuable contribution is made by the churches and by many other voluntary organisations. Children's homes run by voluntary organisations (with some 12,000 places in Great Britain) are required to be registered under the Children Act in England and Wales, in Scotland under the Social Work (Scotland) Act and in Northern Ireland under the Children and Young Persons Act. Arrangements for the care of children and their accommodation are subject to inspection by social work service officers of the Department of Health and Social Security, the Welsh Office, the Scottish Education Department and the Northern Ireland Department of Home Affairs.

Voluntary bodies concerned with the welfare of children in their own homes include local family casework agencies and the Family Service Units. The National Society for the Prevention of Cruelty to Children and its Scottish counterpart maintain inspectors and visitors to investigate reported cruelty or neglect and to undertake preventive work with families.

ADOPTION
Provision for legal adoption was first made in England and Wales in 1926, in Northern Ireland in 1929 and in Scotland in 1930. About 25,000 adoption orders are made annually by the courts in Great Britain and some 500 in Northern Ireland. Adoption is now regulated by the Adoption Act 1958 in Great Britain and by the Adoption Act (Northern Ireland) 1967 in Northern Ireland. The Registrars-General keep registers of adopted children; adoption societies (over 70 in all) must be registered with the local authority (in Northern Ireland, the Department of Home Affairs). Since 1959 local authorities have had the power to act as adoption agencies and increasingly do so.

Since 1968 the number of adoptions registered in Britain has declined. This trend has been partly due to the increasing number of unmarried mothers who decide to keep their babies as a result of changing attitudes to illegitimacy and also to increased state assistance to unmarried mothers. At the same time there is a growing tendency for people to offer to adopt a handicapped child and it is much easier than formerly to place a coloured child.

The report of the Departmental Committee on the Adoption of Children published in October 1972 (see Reading List p 113) has proposed changes in the law relating to adoption. Among them is a recommendation for a new procedure to enable a mother to relinquish her parental rights at an early stage, thereby freeing the prospective parents from the fear that the child might be reclaimed.

The report also recommends that local authorities should have a duty to ensure that a comprehensive adoption service is available throughout their area, and that the responsibility for registering voluntary adoption societies should be transferred from local authorities to central Government.

CHILDREN IN TROUBLE

THE CHILDREN AND YOUNG PERSONS ACT 1969 (for England and Wales) provides for the care and treatment of juvenile offenders[1] and gives local authorities wider responsibilities for undertaking, through social workers, inquiries and consultations with parents, schools and the police, and for the supervision of a child or young person alleged to be an offender and in need of care or control. No child under 10 years of age can be held criminally responsible in England and Wales; the minimum age for prosecution is 12 years (care proceedings replace criminal proceedings if a child aged between 10 and 12 years commits an offence). Juveniles charged with offences or brought before the court as being in need of care or control are dealt with in a juvenile court unless they are charged with homicide or certain grave crimes or are jointly charged with an adult. Every juvenile court must be constituted of not more than three justices and must, except in certain special circumstances, include a man and a woman. In Scotland the age of criminal responsibility is 8 years, but no child can be prosecuted for an offence other than at the instance of the Lord Advocate. Children under 16 years who have committed an offence or need care and protection are generally brought before an informal children's hearing.

The principal orders available to the juvenile courts in England and Wales in both care and criminal proceedings are: (a) a care order, which commits the child to the care of the local authority, (b) a supervision order (usually valid for three years or less) under which a child will normally remain at home under the supervision of the local authority or a probation officer (see p 89), (c) an order requiring a parent or guardian to enter into a recognisance to take proper care of the child or young person and to exercise proper control over him, and (d) a hospital or guardianship order in accordance with the Mental Health Act 1959. In criminal proceedings the courts may also impose fines, order payment of compensation, grant a conditional or absolute discharge, make an attendance centre or detention centre order (see below) or commit a young offender to the Crown Court with a view to borstal training if over 15 years of age.

Attendance Centres

Sixty attendance centres have been established in England and Wales for boys between the ages of 10 and 17 found guilty of offences for which older people could be sentenced to imprisonment. Boys ordered to attend must do so during their spare time on Saturday mornings or afternoons; they may be required to attend for up to three hours on any one occasion and for a total of not less than 12 hours (with certain exceptions) and not more than 24. The activities include physical training and instruction in handicrafts or some other practical subject. Efforts are made at the centres to induce the boys to join a youth club or other suitable organisation.

In Northern Ireland there is one attendance centre; it operates on the same

---

[1]The Act also provides for children brought before a court who are neglected, exposed to moral danger, beyond the control of parents, or playing truant from school.

lines as the centres in England and Wales, but caters for boys between the ages of 12 and 17.

Detention Centres

Detention centres provide a means of training, and are intended to deter from further crime, young offenders for whom a long period of residential training does not seem necessary but who cannot be taught respect for the law by such measures as fines or probation. In England and Wales five junior centres are available for boys of not less than 14 and under 17, and 13 senior centres for young men aged 17 and under 21. In Scotland there is one senior centre. Detention centre orders in England and Wales may be for not less than three and not more than six months for those over 17; if consecutive sentences are passed, the total term may not exceed nine months at any one time. Remission of up to one-third of the sentence may be earned for good conduct. In Scotland the fixed period for all detention centre sentences is three months and the age ranges from 16 to 21.

The regime at detention centres, which is brisk and firm, with strong emphasis on hard work and high standards of behaviour, provides a normal working week of 44 hours, including one hour daily devoted to physical training. Boys of compulsory school age have day-time and evening classes, and further education is provided for others in the evenings. Nearly all young offenders discharged from detention centres are subject to statutory supervision for 12 months.

Borstal Training

The borstal training system, which is available for offenders who have reached the age of 15 but are not yet 21 (16 to 21 in Scotland and Northern Ireland), consists of different borstals specialising in different types of young offender, classified according to such criteria as age, intelligence and criminal sophistication. There are also a few borstals for special purposes, such as allocation or recall. In England, Wales and Northern Ireland the period of training ranges from six months to two years and is followed, in England and Wales, by supervision for two years and in Northern Ireland for one year from the date of release. In Scotland, where there is no minimum period of detention, the maximum is two years and the supervision period is for one year from the date of release. The system is essentially remedial and educational, based on personal training by a carefully selected staff. Emphasis is placed on vocational training in skilled trades; there is much freedom of movement and many borstals are open establishments.

Other Measures

In addition to the above-mentioned establishments to which young offenders can be sent directly by a court, local authorities also have the power to place young people in the following institutions.

Approved Schools and Remand Homes

Approved schools and remand homes are among the establishments being integrated into the system of community homes described on p 38. Over 70 approved schools, together with the 61 former remand homes provided by local authorities, became community homes on 1 April 1973; the remainder of the schools will become community homes by 31 March 1974. Since January 1971[1] courts have been empowered to commit or remand to the care of a local authority; community homes and the remaining approved schools are among the establishments available to local authorities for children in their care. The equivalent institutions for young offenders in Scotland are residential social work schools, the cost of which is shared between the Government and local authorities.

Youth Treatment Centres

For children who are too severely disturbed and disruptive to be treated successfully in approved schools or other existing child care establishments but who do not need treatment in hospital, three new establishments, to be known as Youth Treatment Centres, are being provided in England and Wales under the Children and Young Persons Act 1969. The first of these centres began to admit children in July 1971. Each centre will have a director and a multi-disciplinary staff, and will provide for both boys and girls. The intended general age range is from 12 to 19, but the upper age limit for the first centre is, for the time being, 16.

Intermediate Treatment

Local authorities will also have a duty under the Children and Young Persons Act 1969 to provide intermediate treatment facilities in accordance with regional schemes which were drawn up during 1972. Intermediate treatment (for which facilities may be provided by voluntary bodies also) is intended for children who have been placed by the juvenile court under the supervision of the local authority or of a probation officer, and may consist either of a stay of not more than 90 days in a residential establishment, or of attendance (not exceeding 30 days in any one year) at specified times and places for the purpose of introducing the child to activities of a recreational, educational or cultural nature or of social value under the charge of a responsible person. This new provision is thus 'intermediate' in the sense that it will make possible new forms of treatment for children in trouble which bridge the gap between removal from home and supervision, unsupported by specific treatment measures, while the child remains at home.

---

[1]Before this date courts had powers to order children to be sent to an approved school or to be detained in a remand home pending a further court appearance.

EDUCATION[1]

THERE ARE OVER 11 million children and young people in full-time attendance at schools, universities, colleges of education and technical colleges in Britain. The great majority of schools, attended by some 95 per cent of school children, and most further education establishments are publicly maintained or assisted. Universities are autonomous self-governing institutions but are also aided from public funds.

The bulk of expenditure on education in Britain comes from public funds although some older-established schools and colleges continue to benefit from private endowments. In 1972–73 estimated total public expenditure on education, including school meals, milk, local libraries and museums, amounted to over £3,250 million (about three times the expenditure in 1962–63), which was 14 per cent of all public expenditure.

The Education Act of 1944 now governs public education in England and Wales. The principal legislation in force in Scotland and in Northern Ireland is the Education (Scotland) Act 1962 and the Education Act (Northern Ireland) 1947.

A ten-year education programme for England and Wales was announced by the Government in December 1972. The proposals involve substantially increased expenditure in five sectors: a new programme of nursery education (see p 48); a larger building programme for the renewal of secondary and special, as well as primary, schools; a larger teaching force to improve further the staffing standards in schools; new measures to improve the pre-service and in-service training of teachers; and the development in higher education of a wider range of opportunities for both students and institutions. Similar proposals have been made for Scotland.

Educational Administration

Educational responsibilities are devolved in varying degrees to ministers of the four countries of Britain: the Secretary of State for Education and Science is responsible for all aspects of education in England, for further education in Wales, and for universities, civil science and the arts throughout Great Britain; the Secretary of State for Wales is responsible for nursery, primary and secondary education in Wales; the Secretary of State for Scotland and the Secretary of State for Northern Ireland have full educational responsibilities in their countries except that the Secretary of State for Scotland is consulted about Scottish universities but is not responsible for them.

Administration of publicly provided schools and further education is divided between the central Government departments (the Department of Education and Science, the Welsh Office, the Scottish Education Department, and the Northern Ireland Department of Education), local education authorities,[2] and various voluntary organisations. The relation between these three groups is based on consultation and co-operation.

---

[1] For fuller information, see COI reference pamphlet *Education in Britain*, R4751.
[2] In Northern Ireland five new education and library boards have been set up to assume responsibility for education when the reorganisation of local government took place in October 1973.

The local education authorities are responsible for the provision of school education and further education. They also provide grants to students proceeding to higher education; in Scotland grants are paid by the Scottish Education Department.

In England and Wales colleges of education (for teacher training) are under the financial and administrative control of local education authorities or voluntary organisations. The organisation of courses is based on university institutes of education. The Scottish colleges of education are financed directly by the Scottish Education Department and administered by independent governing bodies; in Northern Ireland they are controlled by the Department of Education or voluntary agencies.

The universities are administratively independent of the central Government departments. The Government exercises its responsibilities in relation to the universities through the University Grants Committee (see p 57). Their governing bodies are appointed according to the terms of their individual charters or statutory provisions.

SCHOOLS

Parents in Britain are required by law to see that their children receive efficient full-time education, at school or elsewhere, between the ages of 5 and 16.

At present there are about 10·5 million school children at 37,490 schools. In England and Wales there were 8·6 million children in publicly maintained schools in 1972 besides 128,730 others at schools receiving direct grants from the Department of Education and Science or the Welsh Office; there were also 422,310 children of all ages at 2,600 independent schools. In Scotland some 1,007,740 children were attending education authority or grant-aided schools and over 17,080 were at independent schools. In Northern Ireland 356,990 children were attending publicly maintained or assisted schools.

In Britain boys and girls are generally taught together in primary schools. Some two-thirds of pupils in maintained secondary schools in England and Wales and nearly one-half in Northern Ireland attend mixed schools. In Scotland nearly all secondary schools are mixed. In the independent sector most of the schools for younger children are co-educational; but of those providing secondary education the majority are either for boys or for girls.

Management

Schools supported from public funds are of three kinds in England and Wales: county schools (the largest group) which are provided and maintained by local education authorities wholly out of public funds; voluntary schools (mostly 'aided' or 'controlled' schools) which have been provided by a voluntary body, usually of a religious denomination[1]; and direct-grant

---

[1] The local education authority is responsible for the running costs of all voluntary schools and for the cost of all building work at controlled schools. Aided schools have more independence than controlled schools and are responsible for part of the cost of external repairs and any building work (see p 51). Over a third of the 28,350 schools maintained by local education authorities in England and Wales are voluntary schools and the majority of these are Church of England schools. There are 2,580 Roman Catholic voluntary schools and smaller numbers belonging to other religious bodies.

schools which are completely independent of local education authorities but receive a grant from the Department of Education and Science or the Welsh Office. These last (the smallest group) are mainly grammar schools; they include some schools of ancient foundation. In Scotland most of the schools supported from public funds are provided by education authorities and are known as public schools (in England this term is used for a type of independent school, see p 50). There are also 27 grant-aided secondary schools comparable to the English direct-grant schools. In Northern Ireland schools managed by education authorities and voluntary schools managed by maintained school committees, boards of governors and individual (usually clerical) managers, are both grant-aided from public funds.

Fees

In England and Wales no fees are charged to parents of children attending maintained schools (that is, over 90 per cent of the school population) and books and equipment are supplied free. In Scotland, education authorities have power to charge fees where this can be done without prejudice to the adequate provision of free school education.

The direct-grant grammar schools in England and Wales and a few of the grant-aided secondary schools in Scotland take pupils paid for by local education authorities as well as those whose fees are paid wholly or partly by parents. In Northern Ireland no fees are charged to parents of children attending grant-aided schools, with the exception of grammar schools, where qualified pupils receive from the education authorities scholarships which cover the whole or most of the fees charged by the school.

Curricula

In England and Wales curricula in maintained schools are under the control of local education authorities, though there is in practice a high degree of devolution to the schools themselves. Teachers may seek help and advice from Her Majesty's Inspectors, who are responsible for the inspection of all schools including independent schools; they review and report on the content and value of the education provided and are available as advisers. Local education authorities also employ inspectors to advise on maintained schools. Further advice and encouragement for school-based research and development is available to teachers through the Schools Council for Curriculum and Examinations. The council, an independent body representative of all educational interests, acts as an advisory body and carries out research and development work on curricula, teaching methods and examinations in primary and secondary schools. In Scotland the function of Her Majesty's Inspectors is in general the same as that of the Inspectorate in England and Wales. The content and balance of the curriculum is kept under continuous review by the Consultative Committee on the Curriculum. Northern Ireland has a Schools Curriculum Committee which works in close liaison with the Schools Council. The Inspectorate of the Department of Education provides help and advice to teachers and is responsible for the inspection and evaluation of the work of all schools.

The schools' freedom to frame their own curricula has facilitated a rapid increase in study and experiment, partly stimulated by the Schools Council and other organisations and partly prompted by the raising of the school-leaving age from 15 to 16 in September 1972. The general purpose is to adapt the curriculum to the everyday life and needs of children and young people.

Religion in Schools

In England and Wales by law all children in county or voluntary schools receive religious instruction and take part in a daily corporate act of worship unless their parents do not wish them to participate. In county schools, and in certain circumstances in voluntary schools, religious instruction of an un-denominational Christian character is given. In all kinds of voluntary school there is opportunity for denominational instruction. In Scotland, subject to safeguards for the individual conscience, religious instruction must be given, but the content is determined by education authorities or, more commonly, by the schools themselves. Roman Catholic children generally have their own schools. In education authority schools in Northern Ireland clergy have a right of access which may be used for denominational purposes. In voluntary schools corporate worship and religious education are controlled by the management authorities.

Health and Welfare of School Children

Physical education, including organised games, is a part of the curriculum of all schools. Those receiving financial assistance from public funds must have the use of a playing field and most secondary schools have a gymnasium. Organised games include tennis, cricket, football, hockey, lacrosse and netball.

The School Health Service provides medical inspection and arranges, usually in co-operation with the National Health Service, for free medical and dental treatment for all children attending schools maintained by local education authorities. Treatment facilities include dental clinics and child guidance centres. From April 1974 responsibility for the medical and dental inspection and treatment functions of the School Health Service will be transferred to the reorganised National Health Service.

Milk (normally one-third of a pint a day) is given free to children of 7 years or under, to children aged between 7 and 12 if they have a medical require-ment, and to pupils in special schools. The School Meals Service provides a midday meal at a subsidised charge (remitted where there is need). The price is gradually being raised to cover the economic cost. About 64 per cent of pupils in England and Wales and about 42 per cent of pupils in Scotland in education authority schools have school midday meals. Education authorities have a duty, under certain conditions, to assist financially in the provision of transport for pupils between home and school.

Priority Areas

The Government has allocated resources under several schemes for the im-provement of educational facilities in 'priority areas'. Special problems in these areas are: poverty, overcrowding and old school buildings. The recom-mendations of the Plowden report (see Reading List p 115) on aid to educa-tional priority areas led to the introduction of a special annual increment for teachers employed in schools of exceptional difficulty and to the allocation of additional funds for school building. Most of the educational resources made available since 1968 under the Urban Aid Programme (see p 95) are being used to provide over 24,000 new nursery places in areas of acute social need in England and Wales. The Community Development Project and the Educational Priority Area project have fostered such innovations as community schools, pre-school experiments and new approaches to adult education. The priority areas will also benefit from the Government's proposals on education (see p 44) which include an increase in expenditure on school building improvement programmes.

Primary Schools

Nursery schools and classes provide informal educational and play facilities. Only a small proportion of children between two and five years old attend these schools but a major expansion of nursery education announced in December 1972 (see p 44) is planned to provide, within ten years, nursery education without charge to those children of three and four whose parents wish them to have it. Compulsory education begins at five when children in England and Wales go to infant schools or departments; at seven they go on to junior schools or departments. At present the usual age of transfer from primary to secondary schools is 11 in England, Wales and Northern Ireland but an increasing number of local authorities in England are establishing 'first' schools for pupils aged 5–8 or 10, and 'middle' schools for pupils aged 8 or 9 to 12 or 13 and 10 to 13. In Scotland, the primary schools take children from 5 to 12, normally having infant classes for children under 7, although in some areas there are separate infant schools.

The content of curricula is very largely a matter for the schools themselves. In England, Wales and Northern Ireland there are no compulsory secular subjects but generally a curriculum includes the teaching of reading, writing, mathematics, English, music, art and handiwork, science and nature study, history and geography. French is taught in an increasing number of schools. Additionally, in Wales, the Welsh language is taught. Where it is the home language of the pupils, Welsh is used as either the main or a secondary medium of teaching in many schools especially in the early years of primary school. In Scotland the scope of the curriculum is similar and provision is made, where appropriate, for the teaching of Gaelic and its use for the purposes of instruction.

One of the most important tasks for schools in Great Britain has been to help immigrant children to improve their knowledge of English, without which they are unable to take advantage of the full school curriculum or the full range of employment opportunities when they leave school. Local education authorities have used a variety of methods to teach English as a second language. In some areas special immigrant language centres have been set up where children from several schools are brought together for intensive language training, either full- or part-time. Some of these centres are equipped with language laboratories and most have teaching machines and other audio-visual materials. In other areas children are withdrawn from their normal classes to receive special help in small groups. Another measure taken is the employment of a team of peripatetic language teachers who visit schools where immigrant pupils are in need of help and who are able to advise other teachers in the schools they visit.

Secondary Schools
England and Wales
The public or state system of education aims to give all children an education suited to their particular abilities. The majority of school children in England and Wales receive their secondary education in schools to which they are allocated after selection procedures at the age of 11. Schools receiving pupils on this basis are: about 1,070 grammar schools providing academic education (including 176 direct-grant grammar schools); some 2,220 secondary modern schools giving a general education with a practical bias; a few secondary technical schools offering a general education related to industry, commerce and agriculture; and schools providing all three, or any two, types of education, in separately organised streams and known as multilateral or bilateral schools.

A third of the maintained secondary school population, however, attend some 1,590 comprehensive schools which take pupils without reference to ability or aptitude and provide a wide range of secondary education for all or most of the children of a district. They can be organised in a number of ways including schools that take the full secondary school age-range from 11 to 18; the middle schools whose pupils move on to senior comprehensive schools at 12 or 13, leaving at 16 or 18; and the comprehensive school with an age-range of 11 or 12 to 16 combined with a sixth-form college for pupils over 16.

Scotland
Secondary education in Scotland is largely organised on comprehensive lines and in 1972, 265,090 pupils (about 80 per cent of all pupils in education authority secondary schools) were in schools with a comprehensive intake. There are also a decreasing number of selective secondary schools which fall mainly into one of three categories or are a combination of all three: (1) schools providing non-certificate courses for pupils likely to leave school at the statutory leaving age of 16; (2) schools which, in addition to non-certificate courses, provide courses leading to the Ordinary grade of the Scottish Certificate of Education; and (3) secondary schools which provide Certificate courses of four, five and six years.

Northern Ireland
In Northern Ireland there are grammar schools and secondary (intermediate) schools, the latter being the equivalent of the secondary modern schools in England and Wales. Some comprehensive type schools exist, and arrangements for transfer between the other types of schools are flexible.

Special Education
Special education is provided for children who require it because of physical or mental disability, including maladjustment, either in ordinary schools or special schools (including hospital schools). There are over 1,690 special schools in Britain, including hospital schools, day and boarding schools. There are also boarding homes for handicapped children attending ordinary schools.

There are ten categories of handicapped pupils in England, Wales and Northern Ireland and nine in Scotland for whom local education authorities must provide special educational treatment: blind, partially sighted, deaf, partially hearing, delicate, educationally subnormal, epileptic, maladjusted, physically handicapped and children suffering from speech defects. There is no separate category for the delicate in Scotland.

Independent Schools

Independent schools in England and Wales receive no grants from public funds but all are open to inspection and must register with the Department of Education and Science (DES) or the Welsh Office which has power to require them to remedy any objectionable features in their premises, accommodation or instruction and to exclude any person regarded as unsuitable to teach in or to be the proprietor of a school. In default, the appropriate Secretary of State can, in effect, close a school, but schools have a right of appeal to an Independent Schools Tribunal against any of the requirements. The schools whose standards are regarded by the DES or the Welsh Office as broadly comparable with those of well-run maintained schools are, on application, granted the status of 'recognised as efficient'. Such schools (1,414 of 2,604 independent schools registered) contain 74·6 per cent of the pupils in independent schools. In Scotland where there are 105 registered schools, the position is generally the same except that there is no 'recognised as efficient' status.

Independent schools cater for pupils of all ages and abilities. They include the preparatory schools and the public schools.[1] The preparatory schools cater mainly for boys from about 8 to 13 years of age who are intending to enter public schools, the largest and most important of the 'recognised as efficient' independent schools. Combined tuition and boarding fees in public schools generally range between £500 and £1,000 a year. There are some 270 public schools about half of which are for girls. The boys' schools in particular include a high proportion of boarding schools and it is among these that some of the most famous schools are numbered.

School-leaving and Secondary School Examinations

The minimum school-leaving age is 16 (raised from 15 in 1972), but the numbers staying on beyond the minimum school-leaving age have shown a steady increase over the past decade.

There is no national school-leaving examination in England and Wales, but secondary school pupils may attempt examinations, in various subjects, leading to the Certificate of Secondary Education (CSE) or the General Certificate of Education (GCE). The CSE is designed for pupils completing five years' secondary education and is normally taken at the age of 16. It is controlled by 14 Regional Examining Boards, consisting mainly of teachers serving in the schools which provide the candidates. The highest grade in the CSE is widely accepted as being of the same standard as a pass at GCE 'Ordinary' level. Control over the scope and standards of the examinations is exercised by the Schools Council (see p 46) to ensure national comparability. The GCE is conducted at 'Ordinary' (O) and 'Advanced' (A) levels. Normally

---

[1]'Public schools' are usually taken to mean those schools in membership of the Headmasters' Conference, the Governing Bodies Association or the Governing Bodies of Girls' Schools Association. Some other schools, mainly direct grant, which are not independent schools, are also represented on these bodies. They should not be confused with the state-supported public schools in Scotland.

candidates taking 'O' level are about 16 years of age, although some take it earlier, at the discretion of their head teacher. Most pupils in grammar, direct grant and independent schools take the 'O' level examination, and so do a number of pupils in comprehensive and other secondary schools.

Passes in various subjects at GCE 'O' level and the equivalent CSE grade are usually considered to be qualifications for entry to courses of further education and training. Since the inception of the CSE the number of passes at the highest grade has increased steadily as the popularity of the examination has grown while the annual number of GCE 'O' level subject passes has increased by nearly half between 1961 and 1972. The 'A' level examination is at the standard for entrance to university and to entry to many forms of professional training. Since 1955 the number of school-leavers obtaining two or more 'A' levels (often regarded as the minimum qualification for university entrance) has more than trebled. Entries for CSE and both levels of the GCE are accepted from candidates at further education establishments and from candidates entering privately.

In Scotland examinations are conducted by the Scottish Certificate of Education Examination Board. School pupils in the fourth year of secondary courses sit an examination at 16 years for the award of passes on the Ordinary grade of the Scottish Certificate of Education, and pupils in the fifth or sixth year are presented for the Higher grade. Passes at the Higher grade are the basis for entry to university or professional training. For those who have completed their main studies at the Higher grade but wish to continue their studies in particular subjects there is a Certificate of Sixth Year Studies.

In Northern Ireland candidates may take the Northern Ireland General Certificate of Education or the Northern Ireland Certificate of Secondary Education.

School Building

Local education authorities and voluntary bodies are responsible, under the general supervision of the central departments, for providing the schools and other buildings needed for public education in their areas. The central departments decide on the size and nature of the authorities' individual programmes in the light of national priorities; they also offer guidance to authorities by means of building bulletins and in other ways.

An extensive school building programme has been carried out resulting in the completion of nearly 14,275 new schools in Britain since 1945; together with extensions, alterations and remodelling of existing state schools, over 7·7 million new places have been provided.

Grants of up to 80 per cent of the approved cost are normally available from the Department of Education and Science or the Welsh Office for the building of new voluntary aided schools and for alterations and external repairs to existing aided schools.

In Northern Ireland capital grants of 80 per cent are available for voluntary schools managed by maintained school committees and voluntary grammar schools which have entered into an agreement under the relevant statutory provisions.

The school building programme has provided for new ideas and methods in design and construction. Industrialised building techniques have been widely adopted. The new schools are light, airy and colourful, with a high standard of finish and generous provision of teaching area and outdoor games space. In primary schools especially, traditional classroom designs are being modified to allow more flexible use of space.

FURTHER EDUCATION

Further education is a broad term used to cover education beyond the secondary stage; it includes much vocational education (full-time, part-time day or evening courses), non-vocational and recreational evening classes, and adult education. Further education advanced courses constitute one of the three sectors of higher education.

Institutions

In England and Wales there are about 630 major establishments of further education including polytechnics, technical colleges, colleges of commerce, colleges of art, and a number of agricultural establishments. They provide both full-time and part-time courses up to the levels of first and higher degrees. There are also over 6,500 evening institutes.

In Scotland there are about 82 local further education colleges offering full- and part-time day courses and a number of evening courses and 13 central institutions for further education doing mainly advanced work.

In Northern Ireland there are 28 institutions of further education.

Finance

Since most further education establishments in Britain are either maintained or aided from public funds, tuition fees are moderate, and nearly always remitted for young people under 18 years of age. Where industrial training is provided by the colleges, charges (the responsibility of the employer) broadly reflect the economic cost of provision. Many full-time students are helped by awards from local education authorities. The awards, generally based on the results of the General Certificate of Education or a corresponding examination, are assessed to cover tuition fees and a maintenance grant, but parents who can afford to contribute towards the cost are required to do so. There are also some scholarships available from endowments, and from particular industries or companies for the most promising of their young workers.

Students

In autumn 1972 there were 344,939 full-time and sandwich-course students (307,000 in England and Wales, 26,077 in Scotland and 11,862 in Northern Ireland) and 1,638,424 part-time students in vocational further education (1·5 million in England and Wales, 115,285 in Scotland and 23,139 in Northern Ireland). The total number of students on advanced courses in England and Wales was about 208,700, in Scotland 19,043, and in Northern Ireland 2,692.

Courses

The courses provided are full-time, sandwich (up to five years in length, generally consisting of alternate periods of about six months of full-time study in a technical college and supervised experience in industry), block release (on similar principles, but with shorter periods in college), day release (generally attendance at a technical college for one day a week during working hours), and evening classes.

Sandwich courses in higher education are becoming increasingly popular. At the lower levels the numbers of day release and block release courses are expanding, and to a large extent replacing evening classes in certain vocational subjects. Many students attend courses in which further education and industrial training are combined.

Technical Courses

There is a wide variety of courses for young people in various trades and occupations, leading to appropriate qualifications at the end of a course of up to five years. Other, more academic, courses lead to the National Certificates and Diplomas approved by joint committees consisting of representatives of education departments, teacher organisations and the appropriate professional bodies.[1] These courses are normally at two levels, ordinary and higher. The Ordinary National Certificate (ONC) courses normally last two years part-time and students usually follow them between the ages of 16 and 19; the level of the certificate is generally considered to approach that of GCE A-level. The Ordinary National Diploma (OND) courses are the full-time or sandwich counterparts of the ONC but involve study to a greater depth. In 1972 some 6,266 ONDs were granted, over nine times the number for 1962. The Higher National Diploma (HND), which requires a further two years' full-time or three years' sandwich study, is recognised, within its more restricted field, as approaching the standard of a pass degree; the Higher National Certificate (HNC), after two further years' part-time study, is lower in standard because it is more narrowly based.

Business and Secretarial Courses

Many technical colleges, evening institutes and independent colleges offer courses in shorthand, typing and book-keeping. Most local technical colleges offer some lower-level work in business and commerce; higher-level work is generally concentrated in colleges with a department of business studies or in specialised colleges of commerce. There are a number of part-time and full-time courses leading to the Certificate or Higher Certificate in Office Studies.

Some business education is related to the specialised examination requirements of various professional bodies; large numbers of the candidates taking such courses do so through correspondence courses. In England, Wales and Northern Ireland there are part-time courses leading to the ONC and HNC in Business Studies. There are also full-time and sandwich courses leading to the OND and HND in Business Studies. In Scotland, similar courses lead to the Scottish National Certificate, the Scottish Higher National Certificate and the Scottish National Diploma in Business Studies awarded by the Scottish Business Education Council.

---

[1] A Technician Education Council and a Business Education Council, proposed in the Haslegrave report (see Reading List, p 115), were set up during 1973 to plan, develop and administer a system of courses in England, Wales and Northern Ireland for technicians in industry, commerce and elsewhere. Similar councils have been set up in Scotland.

Adult Education

Adult education is generally taken to mean courses of non-vocational education for people over 18.[1] In 1972 some 2 million people registered for these courses which were provided by local education authorities, various voluntary bodies, of which the Workers' Educational Association (WEA) is the most notable, certain residential colleges, and the adult education ('extra-mural') departments of universities.

The residential colleges, the university departments and the voluntary bodies, such as the WEA, are recognised as competent to provide adult education and receive Government grants. So do various national bodies which promote educational activities of a non-political kind, such as the National Federation of Women's Institutes and the National Council of Young Men's Christian Associations. Many of these bodies also receive grants from local education authorities for services rendered locally.

A major part of adult education is provided by local education authorities. Most of it is on a part-time basis, mainly in evening institutes (day schools used by adults in the evening) and also in colleges of further education, schools of art, adult education centres, community centres, literary institutes and youth clubs. About 1·8 million students attended local authority adult education classes in 1972. There are about 30 short-term residential colleges or centres in England and Wales maintained or aided by local education authorities, providing courses varying in length between a weekend and a fortnight. Many of the courses are practical, but there are widespread opportunities for academic study.

The village colleges pioneered in Cambridgeshire and variously adapted in Cumberland, Monmouthshire, Leicestershire, Peterborough and Somerset are secondary schools planned also as cultural community centres, providing educational, social and cultural opportunities for adults in mainly rural areas. Community centres in general have a more social character and, though aided by the local education authorities, are usually managed by voluntary community associations many of which are affiliated to the National Federation of Community Associations. The training of community centre wardens is linked with that of youth workers (see p 63).

Residential colleges (six in England and Wales, one in Scotland) provide courses of one or two years, some of which lead to a diploma. The colleges aim at providing a liberal education and do not apply academic entry tests.

In general, courses at the highest levels in liberal studies are provided by the extra-mural departments of the universities, many of which have full-time staff appointed for this purpose and can also call on the services of other members of the university staff; and by the WEA, which also employs organising tutors and works closely with the university extra-mural departments. In 1971–72 over 302,280 students in Britain attended such courses. Similar work is promoted in some education authority centres.

The National Institute of Adult Education provides in London a centre of information, research and publication for adult education, as well as a channel of co-operation and consultation for the many organisations in England and

---

[1]Recommendations for changes in the provision of adult education in England and Wales, made by a committee of inquiry (see Reading List, p 115), are being considered by the Government. A similar committee of inquiry for Scotland is expected to report in 1974.

Wales which are interested in this subject. It is mainly financed by contributions from local education authorities and assisted by a grant from the Department of Education and Science. The Scottish Institute of Adult Education is the corresponding body in Scotland.

In Northern Ireland extra-mural departments of the Queen's University of Belfast and the New University of Ulster organise and staff adult education classes which are supplemented by classes organised by various non-official bodies. The WEA is responsible for classes at other than university level and receives grants from the Department of Education.

TEACHERS

Teachers are appointed by local education authorities or school governing bodies or managers. In 1972 there were about 431,390 full-time and 52,180 part-time (equivalent to 24,766 full-time) teachers in publicly maintained schools in Britain, an average of one teacher to 21·8 pupils. The supply of teachers is increasing rapidly and the pupil-teacher ratio is improving each year. Increasing numbers of university graduates are turning to teaching. In 1972 there were 65,260 full-time teachers in grant-aided establishments of further education in Britain, and many more part-time teachers. There is also an increased use of teachers' aides (helpers) particularly in primary schools, while the rapid growth in the number of teachers' centres (over 600) has helped the spread of new ideas in teaching practice. Most teachers in technical colleges have had industrial and professional experience.

There are national salary scales for teachers in schools and other educational institutions maintained from public funds in England and Wales, in Scotland, and in Northern Ireland.

Teaching Aids and Educational Techniques

In 1972–73 the British Broadcasting Corporation (BBC) broadcast 82 radio series for schools including nine regional series for Wales, eight for Scotland, and four for Northern Ireland. These programmes were used by about 32,000 schools. Television reached some 27,000 schools and the BBC and the Independent Broadcasting Authority between them transmitted 82 series of educational programmes, most of which were repeated.

Radio provides a great variety of educational programmes for adults, both vocational and non-vocational; most of them are grouped in an hourly study programme on five nights a week. Television programmes for similar audiences are mostly shown on Saturday and Sunday mornings and in the evening during the week. There have also been a number of experimental projects sponsored between the BBC, some of the independent television companies, universities and local education authorities. (For the Open University, see p 57.)

A number of other audio-visual aids are in use throughout the educational system. Most universities and a high proportion of colleges of education use closed-circuit television; it is also used increasingly in further education colleges and schools—the Inner London Education Authority's system links about 1,400 educational establishments and is one of the world's biggest networks. There are about 1,700 language laboratories in use in schools in England and Wales.

Schools and colleges co-ordinate different methods of audio-visual presentation, including radio, television, films, colour slides, wall charts, maps, models and tape recordings. For example, the BBC's 'Radiovision' programmes for schools use coloured film strips in conjunction with a tape recording of the broadcast. The Council for Educational Technology for the United Kingdom (formerly the National Council for Educational Technology) and the Educational Foundation for Visual Aids advise all bodies connected with education and with training in industry and in the Services on the use of audio-visual aids.

HIGHER EDUCATION

The system of higher education includes universities, polytechnics, colleges of education and advanced courses at various colleges in the further education system. There has been a rapid expansion in higher education in the last decade; the numbers in full-time higher education in Britain have increased from 198,200 in 1961 to 472,900 in 1971. (Advanced courses are dealt with on p 59 and higher education in Northern Ireland on p 60.)

Universities

There are 44 universities (not counting the Open University) in Britain, compared with 17 in 1945. Although the Government is responsible for providing about 90 per cent of universities' income it does not control their work or teaching nor does it have direct dealings with the universities. The grants are distributed by the University Grants Committee, a body appointed by the Secretary of State for Education and Science to advise her on state aid to the universities; its members are drawn from the academic and business worlds.

The English universities are: Aston[1] (Birmingham), Bath,[1] Birmingham, Bradford,[1] Bristol, Brunel[1] (London), Cambridge, City[1] (London), Durham, East Anglia,[1] Essex,[1] Exeter, Hull, Keele, Kent at Canterbury,[1] Lancaster,[1] Leeds, Leicester, Liverpool, London, Loughborough,[1] Manchester, Newcastle upon Tyne, Nottingham, Oxford, Reading, Salford,[1] Sheffield, Southampton, Surrey,[1] Sussex,[1] Warwick[1] and York.[1] The federated University of Wales includes five university colleges, the Welsh National School of Medicine, and the University of Wales Institute of Science and Technology. The Scottish universities are: Aberdeen, Dundee,[1] Edinburgh, Glasgow, Heriot-Watt[1] (Edinburgh), St Andrews, Stirling,[1] and Strathclyde[1] (Glasgow). In Northern Ireland there is Queen's University, Belfast, and the New University of Ulster[1] in Coleraine.

The Universities of Oxford and Cambridge date from the twelfth and thirteenth centuries and the Scottish Universities of St Andrews, Glasgow, Aberdeen and Edinburgh from the fifteenth and sixteenth centuries. All the other universities were founded in the nineteenth or twentieth centuries.

There are five other institutions where the work is of university standard: the University of Manchester Institute of Science and Technology; the two postgraduate business schools which are supported jointly by industry and the Government—the Manchester Business School and the London Graduate

---

[1]Has received its charter since 1960.

School of Business Studies; Cranfield Institute of Technology for mainly postgraduate work in aeronautics and other subjects; and the Royal College of Art.

The Government has established the Open University to provide part-time degree and other courses, using a combination of television and radio broadcasts, correspondence courses and summer schools, together with a network of viewing and listening centres. No formal academic qualifications are required to register for these courses, but the standards of its degrees (which are awarded on a system of credits for each course completed) are the same as those of other universities. The university is financed by fees and a direct grant from the Department of Education and Science. The first courses began in January 1971, and in July 1973 some 38,000 students were following courses.

University Finance

In spite of the large sums of public money spent on universities they have remained autonomous institutions, due largely to the existence of the University Grants Committee (UGC). The UGC acts as a link between the Government from which it receives a block grant and the universities to which it allocates this grant. In this way the Government contributes about 90 per cent towards both the current income of universities and towards their capital programmes for building work, purchasing sites and properties, professional fees and furniture and equipment. Further sums are raised by the universities themselves.

In Great Britain the recurrent grants for the academic year 1973–74 are estimated to be about £317 million. Capital grants are expected to be about £47 million. Total public expenditure on universities rose from £4 million in 1945 to £400 million in 1972–73. The Comptroller and Auditor General has access to the books and records of the UGC and the universities to check that the funds entrusted to the universities are efficiently administered. He cannot question policy decisions or those reached on academic grounds.

Studies and Degrees

Courses in arts and science are offered by most universities. Imperial College, London, the University of Manchester Institute of Science and Technology and some of the newer universities concentrate on technology although they also offer a number of courses in social studies, modern languages and other non-technological subjects. About 45 per cent of full-time university students in Great Britain are taking arts or social studies courses and 41 per cent science and technology: about 10 per cent are studying medicine, dentistry and health, and the remainder agriculture, forestry, veterinary science, architecture and town and country planning.

University degree courses generally extend over three or four years, though in medicine, dentistry and veterinary science five or six years are required. The first degree of Bachelor (Master in the arts faculties of the older Scottish universities) is awarded on the completion of such a course, depending on satisfactory examination results. Further study or research is required at the modern universities for the degree of Master and by all universities for that of Doctor. Actual degree titles vary according to the practice of each university. A uniform standard of degree throughout the country is ensured by having external examiners on all examining boards. In the last decade there has been a tendency for degree courses to become more broadly based in subject matter, particularly in the new universities.

University teaching combines lectures, practical classes (in scientific subjects) and small group teaching in either seminars or tutorials.

Most members of the academic staffs devote time to research and at all universities there are postgraduate students engaged in research.

Students

Admission to the universities is by examination and selection; there is no religious test and no colour bar. Women are admitted on equal terms with men but at Cambridge their numbers may be limited by ordinance. The general proportion of men to women students is about three to one; at Oxford it is over four to one, and at Cambridge seven to one. Over a third of all full-time university students in Britain are living in colleges and halls of residence, slightly under a half are in lodgings, and the remainder live at home.

Despite recent expansion programmes, applications for places at universities for arts studies still exceed the number available. Prospective candidates for nearly all the universities apply for places through the Universities Central Council on Admissions. The only students to apply directly are applicants to the Open University and British candidates who apply only to the universities of Glasgow, Aberdeen and Strathclyde.

In 1972–73 there were about 241,000 full-time university students in Great Britain including 45,000 postgraduates. In 1971–72 there were some 26,000 part-time students. Some 22,000 home and overseas candidates were also registered in 1973 for London University's external first degree examinations.

Staff

In 1971–72 there were about 29,000 full-time university teachers in Great Britain; about 12 per cent of them were professors. The ratio of staff to students was about one to eight, one of the most favourable in the world.

Teacher Training

Teachers in maintained schools must hold qualifications approved by the education departments. In England and Wales the majority qualify by undertaking a three-year course at a college of education.[1] Some college students obtain a degree—Bachelor of Education (B.Ed)—and a professional qualification by means of a four-year course. An additional year's compulsory professional training for people with degrees and certain other specialist qualifications, hitherto entitled to teach without further training, is gradually being introduced. In Scotland all teachers in secondary schools must be graduates (or have equivalent qualifications) and must have taken a course of teacher training but primary school teachers may qualify by taking a three-year course at a college of education. The General Teaching Council has almost complete powers over the profession excluding salary matters but including the function of maintaining a register of qualified teachers.

[1] The Government has announced proposals for changes in the system of teacher training (see p 44) based on the recommendations made by the James committee of inquiry (see Reading List, p 116).

In England and Wales there are 152 colleges of education, 14 of which are for day students only, 7 departments of education in polytechnics, 30 university departments of education, 4 colleges for training teachers for technical institutions and 13 art teacher training centres. In October 1972 there were about 114,000 students in colleges and departments of education outside universities (including over 7,000 in day colleges), some 7,500 in university departments of education, and 3,000 in colleges of education (technical) and art teacher training centres. In Scotland there are 10 colleges of education; the number of students in training in 1972–73 was over 14,800.

The education departments, universities, local authorities and other bodies provide a variety of short in-service training courses for practising teachers.

Advanced Courses in Further Education

In 1972–73 over 227,743 students in Great Britain were taking advanced courses other than in universities and colleges of education in a wide variety of subjects including architecture, art and design, catering, engineering, natural sciences and business studies. An increasing proportion of the students were taking courses leading to the awards of the Council for National Academic Awards. The council has power to award degrees and other academic qualifications, comparable in standard with those granted by universities, to students who successfully complete approved courses of study in establishments which do not have the power to award their own degrees. In 1972–73 there were 498 courses being followed by about 34,868 students. These courses were mainly in science and technology but included the arts, social studies, business studies and law.

In England and Wales higher education provision outside universities and colleges of education is being concentrated within 30 major national institutions named 'polytechnics'. They are comprehensive institutions providing all types of courses (full-time, sandwich, and part-time) at all levels of higher education. By 1973, all 30 polytechnics had been formally designated. In Scotland similar provision is made in 10 central institutions and a few further education colleges managed by education authorities.

Management studies are provided by universities, polytechnics and other further education colleges, by individual companies and by trade and industrial federations. (For the two postgraduate business schools, see p 56.) Certain independent colleges specialise in management training. Many universities have introduced management studies into the curriculum and courses for the postgraduate Diploma in Management Studies are run by about 40 further education colleges. In Scotland courses leading to the Certificate of Business Administration are provided for students in junior supervisory positions.

Awards

Awards to enable students to undertake higher education are made under one of the most generous grant systems in the world. It is national policy that no boy or girl should be prevented by lack of means from taking an advanced course at a university or elsewhere. As a result, over 90 per cent of students in higher education in Great Britain are aided from private or public funds.

In England, Wales and Scotland most adequately qualified British students can obtain awards from public funds in order to attend full-time at a university, college of education or major further education establishment. In England and Wales local education authorities provide awards. In Scotland students' allowances for advanced courses are granted by the Scottish Education Department. The amount of these awards depends upon the income of the student and his parents. Grants for postgraduate study are offered annually by the Department of Education and Science, the Research Councils and the Scottish Education Department.

Northern Ireland

Two institutions provide university education in Northern Ireland—Queen's University of Belfast and the New University of Ulster, Coleraine. The New University consists of four schools (biological studies, social and economic studies, physical sciences and humanities) and an education centre with the status of a school. Technological studies are provided at Queen's University, Belfast, in addition to a wide range of courses in other faculties. In October 1972 there were 5,830 students at Queen's University and 1,640 at the New University. Government grants to the universities are made by the Department of Education which first seeks the advice of the University Grants Committee.

Higher education outside the universities is mainly centred in a new polytechnic called Ulster College which has 1,505 full-time and 1,791 part-time students.

Teacher training takes place in the two university education departments, three colleges of education, the Ulster College and one technical college. In 1972–73 there were about 3,191 students in training. The principal courses are three-year (certificate) and four-year (Bachelor of Education) but there are also one-year courses for graduates or holders of other appropriate qualifications. University and further education scholarships are awarded by local education authorities and postgraduate awards and teacher-training scholarships by the Department of Education, the conditions of award being the same as those for Great Britain.

EDUCATIONAL RESEARCH

Research into the theory and practice of education and the organisation of educational services is supported financially by the education departments, local education authorities, philanthropic organisations, universities and teachers' associations. The Schools Council and the Social Science Research Council are additional channels for Government support.

The major institute undertaking research in education, outside the universities, is the National Foundation for Educational Research, an autonomous body which derives its income mainly from corporate members, including local education authorities, teachers' organisations and universities and from an annual grant from the Department of Education and Science. There are also the Scottish Council for Research in Education and the Northern Ireland Council for Educational Research.

Some research is undertaken at colleges of education and polytechnics and by a few independent research organisations.

Among philanthropic organisations that provide generously for research are the Nuffield Foundation, the Ford Foundation, the Gulbenkian Foundation, the Leverhulme Trust, the Bernard van Leer Foundation, the Rockefeller Foundation, the Carnegie United Kingdom Trust, the Wolfson Foundation and the Foundation for Management Education.

THE YOUTH SERVICE[1]

THE AIM of the youth service in Britain is to encourage the development of young people by helping them to broaden their interests, to enjoy recreational pursuits, and to mix socially in their leisure time.

The service (which in Scotland forms part of the Youth and Community Service) is provided by local education authorities and voluntary organisations, in co-operation with the Government education departments. Membership of youth groups is voluntary and groups vary greatly in their activities, there being no attempt to impose uniformity or to create anything in the nature of a national youth movement.

Organisation and Finance

The education departments formulate broad policy objectives for the service and encourage their achievement through financial assistance and advice. They make known the Government's attitude by means of circulars to local education authorities and through contacts between departmental officials and representatives of the authorities and the voluntary organisations. Ministers in Scotland and Northern Ireland are advised on the finance and development of the service by councils representing all those concerned in youth work. Financially the education departments assist voluntary organisations through grants towards their costs for central administration and building projects.

Almost all local education authorities assist local voluntary groups by lending premises and equipment and some contribute to their capital and running costs. To supplement the work of voluntary groups, many authorities now construct and run youth centres and clubs; in Great Britain there are several thousand youth centres fully run by local education authorities. Most authorities have appointed youth committees on which official and voluntary bodies are represented, and employ youth organisers to help in the promotion and encouragement of youth work. In 1972–73, local education authorities spent an estimated £21·3 million on the youth service in England and Wales and £601,465 in Scotland.

Although the number of local education authority youth clubs and centres is growing, national voluntary organisations still promote the largest share of youth activities through local groups, which raise most of their day-to-day running expenses by their own efforts; these have an estimated membership in Britain of 5·5 million. Some 45 national youth organisations and 34 local co-ordinating bodies are full members of the National Council for Voluntary Youth Services (NCVYS), a consultative body which takes action only in the name and with the consent of its member bodies; a further 15 organisations are observers. In Scotland, Wales and Northern Ireland there are similar representative bodies.

Among the largest of the voluntary youth organisations belonging to the NCVYS are the Scouts and Girl Guides Associations (with 492,319 and 772,092 members), the National Association of Youth Clubs (357,150), the

---

[1]For fuller information, see COI reference pamphlet *The Youth Service in Britain*, R5506.

National Association of Boys' Clubs (174,410), the Youth Hostels Association (234,000) and the Methodist Association of Youth Clubs (130,000).

Certain pre-Service organisations for boys, which provide facilities for social, educational and physical development along with training for possible entry to the armed forces, are also members of the NCVYS; they are assisted financially by the Ministry of Defence.

Membership

Local education authority youth groups in England and Wales normally cater for young people of both sexes mainly in the 14–20 age-range. Voluntary organisations frequently cater for young people on a single-sex basis and their membership often covers a wider age-range. An official survey published in 1972 on the youth service and similar provisions (see Reading List, p. 116) showed that some two-thirds of young people aged 14–20 were members of a club or association (including associations attached to schools, colleges and universities, and places of work). The survey also indicated that 68 per cent or more were or had been members of a youth club. A smaller proportion of girls than boys take part in youth club activities and the main involvement is between the ages of 14 and 16.

Training of Youth Workers

Most youth workers operate part-time and many of them are unpaid. Part-time workers usually have no professional qualification in youth work but many have allied qualifications, for instance as teachers, and a large number attend short courses and conferences on youth work.

In England and Wales, for full-time youth workers there is a basic two-year training undertaken in conjunction with the training of community centre wardens. Provided at colleges of education and further education, the course leads to a professional qualification. In addition a number of colleges of education provide a study of youth work as a principal or subsidiary subject within a teacher-training course. In Scotland one- and three-year courses are provided at certain colleges of education.

Other Organisations Concerned with Young People

There are in Britain a number of organisations, which, although primarily concerned with the welfare and out-of-school pursuits of young people, operate in a context broader than that of any individual youth movement. Among the most important are the Sports Councils for England, Wales, Scotland and Northern Ireland, which provide practical and advisory services for many youth organisations; the National Playing Fields Association, which advises local authorities and sports organisations on the acquisition, layout, construction and use of sports grounds; and the Outward Bound Trust, which maintains six sea and mountain schools in Britain offering full-time residential courses designed to encourage a sense of adventure, responsibility, confidence and achievement.

The Duke of Edinburgh's Award Scheme, which operates through bodies such as local authorities, schools, youth organisations and industrial firms, is designed as a challenge to young people to reach certain standards in leisure-time activities with the voluntary assistance of adults. Some 180,000 young people between the ages of 14 and 21 from Britain and other Commonwealth countries took part in the scheme in 1972. There are three awards—Bronze, Silver and Gold—for each of which young people must attempt activities in four out of five sections: service; interests; expeditions; and either physical activity or design for living.

The King George's Jubilee Trust is a charitable body which, since its creation in 1935, has distributed more than £2·6 million in grants to voluntary youth organisations and towards experimental youth projects.

Community Service by Young People

There has been considerable growth in voluntary service by young people to those in need in the community, for example, the elderly, the sick, the mentally ill and the handicapped. Organisations such as International Voluntary Service, Task Force and Community Service Volunteers receive grants from the Department of Education and Science, and through them thousands of young people are doing full- or part-time voluntary work for the community. Many schools organise community service activities as part of the curriculum. Young people also play an active part in fund-raising for charitable organisations.

The Government established the Young Volunteer Force Foundation in 1968 as an independent body to advise interested organisations in England and Wales on methods of involving young people in providing service to the community. The foundation is grant-aided by the Government and employs teams of young people who are available on request to assist such bodies as local authorities, voluntary organisations and hospital boards in encouraging and promoting voluntary service. In Scotland, a similar organisation, 'Enterprise Youth', has been established to co-ordinate and promote voluntary service to the community.

EMPLOYMENT AND TRAINING SERVICES

THE STATE provides a number of employment services many of which have a social as well as an economic purpose. In particular, some of the placement and training services and the measures to secure adequate standards of safety, health, amenity and comfort in places of work may be regarded as social services. The Department of Employment (DE) is ultimately responsible for these functions in Great Britain, and the Department of Health and Social Services in Northern Ireland.

A Manpower Services Commission is set up to develop and co-ordinate the Government's employment and training services, under the Employment and Training Act 1973.

EMPLOYMENT SERVICES

The main Government employment services are provided in Great Britain through a national network of 'Jobcentres' and local employment offices of the DE. The services in Northern Ireland are run on similar lines but there are some variations related to the much smaller area of administration.

The 'Jobcentres' and employment offices provide a comprehensive service for employers needing staff and for people, whether or not already in employment, seeking jobs. Information and advice on any employment problem is available to all and expert advice on careers and employment may be obtained from occupational guidance units. Use of the service is voluntary. Employers and individuals alike remain free to use general or specialised fee-charging private employment agencies and direct recruitment by advertisement or personal introduction.

The DE's local offices handle the full range of occupations and deal with full-time, part-time and temporary vacancies. Details of unfilled vacancies (or of people seeking jobs) can be circulated quickly in the 'travel to work' area, or more widely if necessary. Local employment committees, on which employers, workers and other local interests are represented, are attached to the employment office network as advisory bodies to secure the full benefit of local knowledge and the close co-operation of employers and workers.

A computerised national matching service for managerial, professional, scientific and technical occupations is provided through Professional and Executive Recruitment. This is an independent service operating from more than 40 offices in the main centres of population. It is free to those who seek appointments through it, but employers who use it are charged a fee.

There are, in addition, a number of specialised employment services available to particular groups of people. Among these are the Youth Employment Service and the Disablement Resettlement Service.

Youth Employment Service

The Youth Employment Service in Great Britain is available to all young people up to the age of 18, or older if they are still at school. Its main functions are to work with careers teachers in schools in providing young people and their parents with information on educational and employment opportunities;

to give vocational guidance to young people in their later years at school; to help young people to find suitable employment and employers to find suitable workers; and to follow up the progress of young people in employment and give them any further help or advice they may need. The Secretary of State for Employment has responsibility for the service and is advised by a National Youth Employment Council. Central administration is the responsibility of the Central Youth Employment Executive which consists of senior officers of the DE and the education departments.

Local education authorities have the option of operating the service in their own areas. Where an authority provides an approved scheme, 75 per cent of its expenses is reimbursed from state funds. Some 143 local authorities covering approximately 80 per cent of the school population operate the service based on their own careers offices. In the remaining parts of the country the service is provided from careers offices of the DE. With the reorganisation of local government in 1974–75 this system will end. From then every local authority will have a duty to make arrangements to provide a vocational guidance service for people attending educational institutions and an employment service for those leaving them.

In Northern Ireland the functions of the Youth Employment Service are similar to those in Great Britain but its organisation is different in that the service is operated by a statutory board composed of representatives of local education authorities and other educational and industrial interests.

Disablement Resettlement Service

The Disablement Resettlement Service is designed to help disabled people to get and keep suitable work. It is available to anyone over school-leaving age who is substantially handicapped. Until the service is taken over by the Manpower Services Commission, the DE is responsible for its administration. It is advised by the National Advisory Council on the Employment of the Disabled, an independent statutory body on which employers and workers are represented; the membership also includes doctors and other people experience in the problems of disablement.

Vocational guidance and help in finding employment is given at local offices by specialised disablement resettlement officers (DROs) who, where necessary, arrange for a course of industrial rehabilitation or training or both. A Register of Disabled Persons is maintained and all employers of 20 or more persons have an obligation to employ a quota (at present 3 per cent for all industries, except shipping in respect of the manning of ships) of registered disabled persons; at present the scheme is under review.

Industrial rehabilitation is provided at 25 units (including one combined medical/industrial rehabilitation unit) run by the DE. Attendance at a unit is voluntary and maintenance allowances are paid. The DE also gives financial help to voluntary organisations operating nine rehabilitation centres.

There are vocational training facilities for the disabled at Government Training Centres, educational institutions and employers' establishments. For the more seriously disabled there are special residential training colleges run by voluntary organisations with the help of the DE. Grants are available to disabled people qualified to undertake study or training for professional or comparable employment.

66

Remploy Ltd, a non-profit-making company, partly supported by public funds, provides sheltered employment for about 8,000 registered severely disabled people who are unlikely to obtain work except under special conditions. The DE helps local authorities and voluntary organisations with the cost of providing facilities for sheltered employment for over 3,000 severely disabled sighted workers and for 2,560 blind workers.

In Northern Ireland, although there is separate legislation, it is the same as that in Great Britain and there is parity of treatment of disabled persons with their counterparts in Great Britain. Administration of the Disabled Resettlement Service is the responsibility of the Northern Ireland Department of Health and Social Services. Remploy has no facilities in Northern Ireland but a similar company, Ulster Sheltered Employment Ltd, provides employment for about 50 seriously disabled people. The Department of Health and Social Services assists local authorities and voluntary organisations with the costs of providing sheltered employment for a number of disabled people.

INDUSTRIAL TRAINING

Most industrial and commercial training has always been carried out by individual employers, but in recent years the Government has taken a number of measures based on the economic need to provide trained manpower to sustain future economic growth and the social need to provide training for workers wishing to change their occupation, who failed for whatever reason to acquire skills immediately after the completion of their education or who found that they had made a wrong choice in their first career.

Government Training Opportunities Scheme

The Government Training Opportunities Scheme to be administered by the Manpower Services Commission is intended to meet the training needs of both employers and individuals. Training is carried out at Government Training Centres and in colleges and employers' establishments. Trainees are paid allowances which vary according to the number of their dependants and their former earnings. Allowances are substantially higher than unemployment benefit. For severely disabled people training is provided at four residential training colleges run by voluntary organisations with Government financial assistance.

Over the next few years the Government plans to expand the scheme substantially. The range of courses is being made much wider and more training places are being provided, so that by 1975, 70,000 people a year will receive training, thereafter increasing as soon as possible to 100,000.

Training Services in the Assisted Areas

The DE provides additional training services specifically for employers in the assisted areas, that is, areas with high unemployment where industrial development is being encouraged by the Government. Departmental courses for supervisors and industrial training instructors, the training of experienced workers in instructional techniques, and the loan of departmental mobile instructors to conduct in-plant training are available to all firms in these areas. Special schemes may also be provided where major redundancies occur in assisted areas and to meet the needs of older workers needing retraining.

SAFETY AND HEALTH OF EMPLOYEES
Safety
Employers have a duty at common law to take reasonable care of their employees and provide a safe system of working, while employees have a duty of care towards each other. In addition, minimum required standards of safety in certain kinds of workplaces or work are laid down under a number of statutes; some of these also deal with health and welfare.

Regulations

About 250,000 industrial premises (factories, warehouses, shipyards, docks and construction sites) come under the Factories Act 1961 (consolidating earlier legislation), which is administered by the DE and enforced by Her Majesty's Inspectorate of Factories, which forms part of the DE. About 750,000 premises are subject to the Offices, Shops and Railway Premises Act 1963, which is also administered partly by the DE; enforcement is shared by Her Majesty's Inspectorates of Factories and of Mines and Quarries, and local authorities.

The Acts and regulations made under them are designed to secure the health, safety and welfare of employees, and deal with such matters as the fencing of machinery; precautions against fire and special risks; the safe condition of the premises; and cleanliness, lighting, temperature and ventilation. Anyone intending to employ other people in industrial or commercial premises to which the Acts apply has to notify the enforcing authority of his intention before he begins to employ people and every fatal accident and every accident causing more than three days' incapacity must be reported. The Factories Act includes provisions for the compulsory notification and investigation of certain dangerous occurrences, for precautions against dangerous substances and about the employment of women and young people.

Comparable provision with appropriate variations covers mines and quarries under the Mines and Quarries Act 1954; two statutes are concerned with agriculture—the Agriculture (Poisonous Substances) Act 1952 and the Agriculture (Safety, Health and Welfare Provisions) Act 1956; and specialised statutes and delegated legislation are concerned with transport—the Railway Employment (Prevention of Accidents) Act 1900, the Merchant Shipping Acts, the Road Traffic Acts and the Air Navigation Order and Regulations.

As with the Factories Act these other provisions are, with some exceptions, enforced through inspectorates—the Mines and Quarries Inspectorate (part of the Department of Trade and Industry (DTI), which is responsible for safety in mines and quarries), the Agricultural Inspectorate of the agricultural departments, and, for railways, the Railway Employment Inspectorate of the Department of the Environment. The DTI is responsible for administering the Merchant Shipping Acts and for safety in air transport (most of the powers in respect of airworthiness are delegated to the Civil Aviation

Education

The library in an infants school. 'Open plan' primary schools emphasise space and enable easy access to be made to all facilities.

A 'middle school'. Middle schools take children from the ages of 8 to 10 until they are 12 or 13.

A junior class in a special school for the deaf.

An English language class at a special centre for young immigrants.

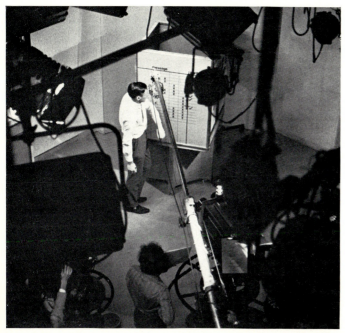

Television technicians recording a mathematics programme for the Open University. Programmes are transmitted twice weekly on the national network of the British Broadcasting Corporation.

New buildings at Stirling University in Scotland.

Health Services

The main entrance to one of London's teaching hospitals.

The operations room of the Ambulance Control Centre in London.

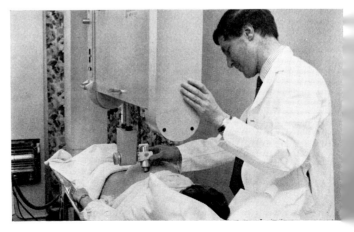

An ultrasonic diagnostic scanner. Ultrasonics can detect abnormalities in soft tissues which are invisible by other techniques.

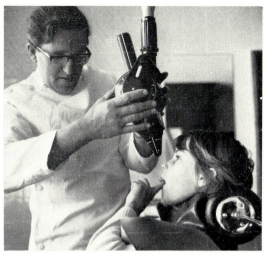

Dental treatment at a children's clinic.

A home nurse visits a patient.

A patient being introduced to a new electrically assisted invalid chair which, like the invalid vehicle to the right of the picture, is provided free under the National Health Service to certain disabled people.

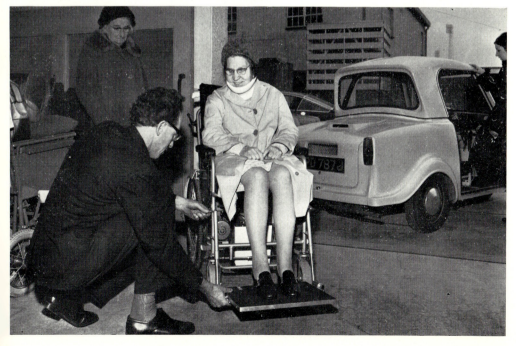

Employment

Instruction in workshop practice at an industrial rehabilitation unit.

New self-service 'Jobcentres', replacing existing employment exchanges throughout Britain, will offer a comprehensive employment service to the community.

Housing

A new local authority housing estate in Coventry.

Old houses in London after rehabilitation.

Voluntary Organisations

A young Task Force volunteer does the shopping for an elderly pensioner.

A playgroup organised by the Save the Children Fund.

Authority and the Department of the Environment is responsible for road and rail transport safety matters. Safety requirements in hotels, places of entertainment or educational establishments are covered by the 1971 Fire Precautions Act or (in respect of their offices and shops) by the Offices, Shops and Railway Premises Act. The DE has no statutory responsibility in regard to safety in workshops or laboratories in educational establishments, though it keeps in touch with university authorities and the education departments.

Other Measures

Transport operators and ministries concerned with road and air travel give high priority to safety measures affecting crews and passengers. Every effort is made to counter the higher risks resulting from rising traffic densities by improving the design of vehicles, transport plant and equipment, by traffic regulation and control of standards of maintenance and by training crews in competency and safety awareness.

To safeguard the many interests which might be adversely affected by the use of chemicals in agriculture and food storage, a voluntary scheme is operated by the Government with the help of an advisory committee and with the full co-operation of the chemical industry.

The National Coal Board has its own safety organisation—a Standing Committee on Safety, a chief safety engineer, and safety engineers at divisions, areas and the largest collieries.

The Promotion of Safety Measures

The DE encourages the development of voluntary central organisation within each industry at national level for the consideration of safety matters and the formulation of policy and accident prevention. Its Factory Inspectorate, besides inquiring into notified accidents and safety aspects of machine design and specification, circulates expert advice by personal exhortation, lectures and literature, and encourages the appointment of safety officers and the formation of works safety committees, and maintains an industrial health and safety centre in London, at which various types of machinery demonstrating the effectiveness of guards are displayed, as well as a wide range of protective clothing and equipment.

Organisations in industry participate also in joint standing and advisory committees appointed by the Secretary of State. Representatives of the Trades Union Congress, the Confederation of British Industry, the nationalised industries and other interests meet on the Industrial Safety Advisory Council under the chairmanship of the Secretary of State. The Royal Society for the Prevention of Accidents (RoSPA) and the British Safety Council are two major national bodies concerned with accident prevention. A number of local accident prevention groups are affiliated to either RoSPA or the British Safety Council. These groups serve as forums where questions of industrial safety can be examined and knowledge of accident prevention exchanged.

Health

Local authorities have power, under the Public Health Acts, to regulate the provision of suitable sanitary accommodation at places of work and to treat workplaces which are dirty or badly ventilated or overcrowded as nuisances, the abatement of which can be enforced. Factories, certain other industrial premises, offices, shops and railway premises must comply with the health and welfare requirements of the Factories Act or the Offices, Shops and Railway Premises Act. These include: the cleanliness of workrooms, adequate ventilation and suitable temperature and lighting, the avoidance of overcrowding and the provision of sanitary accommodation, and the protection of workers against inhaling harmful dust or fumes; and the provision of washing facilities, lockers or other accommodation for outdoor clothing, drinking water, first aid and seats. Appropriate measures concerning safety in other types of work, for example, agriculture, are also prescribed.

Legislation, besides forbidding employment of children under 13 years of age, forbids the employment of children who have not reached the statutory minimum school-leaving age (16) in any industrial undertaking; of women and young people underground in mines and in certain other dangerous occupations (for example, certain processes connected with lead manufacture); and of women in factories and workshops within four weeks after childbirth. It also limits and defines the permissible hours of work for women and young people in some employments. Local authorities, moreover, have wide powers under the Children and Young Persons Acts 1933–63 as well as the Education Acts 1944–62, to regulate hours and conditions of employment of children within their areas.

The Employment Medical Advisory Service, set up in February 1973 under the Employment Medical Advisory Service Act 1972, is available to give advice free of charge to employers, employees, trade unions, general practitioners and others on the medical aspects of any employment problem. The service has a national network of over 100 doctors known as employment medical advisers who specialise in occupational medicine, and who are based in the main industrial centres. They are assisted by occupational health nurses.

The service has two main priorities: first, the carrying out of periodic medical examinations of workers engaged on certain hazardous trades which are covered by the Factories Act; and secondly, helping to advise young people starting work on the medical aspects of their choice of employment.

Employment medical advisers work closely with school medical officers and careers officers to help advise young people before they leave school about their choice of work. In addition, employers covered by the Factories Act are required to notify the local careers office within seven days whenever a young person starts work.

The service is also responsible for advising the DE's placing, training and disablement resettlement services and provides medical supervision in the DE's industrial rehabilitation units. It works in close collaboration with the Factory Inspectorate, liaises closely with the inspectorate's industrial hygiene unit, maintains a central reference laboratory, works with the national health service, and has available to it the full range of national health service laboratory and X-ray services.

It also collaborates with Government agencies such as the Medical Research Council as well as with works medical services which are provided voluntarily by many employers.

Health Services in Industry

It is estimated that there are about 400 factories with doctors providing full-time medical cover and about 4,000 factories with part-time medical cover. In addition, several thousand nurses are employed in industry. The big employers, including the State and the boards of nationalised industries, have taken the lead, but a number of smaller factories also provide medical services and in a few cases have joined together in group medical services. It is estimated that about one-third of all employees in factories are covered by full- or part-time works medical officers. The Secretary of State is advised on measures to further the development of health services in workplaces covered by the Factories Act by the Industrial Health Advisory Committee, which includes members nominated by the Confederation of British Industry, the Trades Union Congress (TUC), the nationalised industries, the British Medical Association, the Royal College of Nursing and other organisations closely concerned with the promotion of industrial health.

Advice and Research

The Factory Inspectorate gives advice on occupational hygiene problems and has an industrial hygiene unit, with laboratory facilities. There are some six centres in Great Britain (including the TUC's Institute of Occupational Health) which undertake studies of particular problems or health risks and also carry out routine physical, chemical and biological tests for industry.

Research facilities are provided by Government agencies such as the Medical Research Council (see p 33); by university faculties of industrial health and social medicine; and by the research departments of various industries and large industrial concerns. Field investigations are carried out by the Factory Inspectorate, which has specialised technical branches.

Other Amenities

An increasing number of firms pay part or all of the cost of recreational facilities. Some have their own rehabilitation centres or support convalescent homes. The provision of low-priced meals at the place of employment has become usual in large undertakings and quite common in smaller ones. Many offices and shops which are unable to provide canteen facilities for their staff have adopted luncheon voucher schemes.

Safety and Health in Northern Ireland

The safety, health and welfare of employees in Northern Ireland have been the subject of legislation which, with some exceptions, is similar to that in Great Britain and is embodied in the Factories Act (Northern Ireland) 1965 and the Office and Shop Premises Act (Northern Ireland) 1966. Many firms voluntarily employ safety officers, and an Industrial Safety Group for the area, supported by representatives of industry, trade unions, insurance companies and public authorities, makes a valuable contribution in the field of industrial accident prevention on similar lines to what is done in Great Britain.

HOUSING[1]

THERE ARE 19·6 million dwellings in Britain: over 17·3 million in England and Wales, 1·8 million in Scotland and 460,000 in Northern Ireland. Nationally the numbers of households and dwellings are about equal, but they are unevenly distributed, and housing shortages persist in the more prosperous commercial and industrial centres, such as London and Birmingham.

The large majority of people in Great Britain—85 per cent in the 1966 sample census—live in houses or bungalows, mostly with gardens; the remainder live in flats or maisonettes, normally in blocks of from two to 20 storeys.

About a half of all dwellings in Britain are owned by their occupiers, some 30 per cent are rented from public housing authorities, and most of the remainder are rented from private landlords. There are variations, however, in the distribution of tenure between the different countries of Britain—in Scotland more than half the dwellings are rented from public authorities—and in different regions and areas of those countries. Private rented accommodation is generally more common in the central districts of large towns, while owner-occupation is more frequent in their outer suburbs and in country areas.

New house construction in Britain is undertaken by both public and private sectors. Of the 330,747 dwellings completed in 1972, nearly two-thirds were provided by private interests, over a third by public authorities, and over 2 per cent by voluntary housing associations and societies. Public housing authorities provide dwellings mainly for renting, while private interests build mainly for sale to owner-occupiers. The construction of private dwellings to rent has dwindled to a very low level.

Over 8 million new dwellings have been built in Britain since 1945, and two families in every five now live in a post-war dwelling. There remain a large number of older dwellings, some of which have been kept in good repair and modernised, while many others—particularly in the centres of cities—are unsatisfactory by modern standards. A survey carried out in 1971 established that out of a total stock of 17·1 million dwellings in England and Wales, some 1·2 million (7 per cent) were unfit, while a further 1·9 million (11 per cent) lacked basic amenities. The demolition of slum dwellings and more advanced standards for new house-building (particularly in the public sector) have, however, led to significant improvements in the general quality of British housing.

ADMINISTRATION AND POLICY

Responsibility for formulating housing policy and supervising the housing programme is borne by the Secretary of State for the Environment in England and by the Secretaries of State for Scotland, Wales and Northern Ireland.

In Great Britain most of the public housing is provided by 1,600 local housing authorities, which are responsible for ensuring that the supply of

[1]For fuller information, see COI reference pamphlets *Housing in Britain*, R5875, and *The New Towns of Britain*, R4506.

housing in their areas is adequate. These are: in England and Wales, the councils of county boroughs, boroughs, urban and rural districts; in London, the Greater London Council, the London borough councils and the Common Council of the City of London; and in Scotland, the town and county councils. Local government reorganisation in 1974 (in England and Wales) and 1975 (in Scotland) will greatly reduce the number of housing authorities. Other public housing authorities in Great Britain are the new town authorities and the Scottish Special Housing Association (SSHA), which was established in 1937 to supplement building by local authorities in Scotland.

The central Government departments specify certain standards for the construction and equipment of all new dwellings; these are enforced by the local authorities. In the public sector, local housing authorities have been freed from Government control over the number and costs of new building. Subsidies are made available to the authorities to assist them with housing costs, and guidance is given on design and layout.

Besides providing public housing, local authorities are involved in many other aspects of housing policy, including paying house improvement grants to the private sector, granting mortgages (see p 76) to owner-occupiers, and carrying out slum-clearance and redevelopment programmes. A growing number are establishing housing advisory centres to provide the public with information on local housing opportunities in both public and private sectors.

In Northern Ireland, the Northern Ireland Housing Executive, a public body established in 1971, has assumed the housing responsibilities previously exercised by local authorities and the Northern Ireland Housing Trust. The executive is taking over the housing functions of the new town development commissions, and is to become the sole public housing authority in Northern Ireland. The executive is aided by a housing council representing each local authority area.

The main objectives of Government housing policy are to secure a decent home for every family at a price within its means, to offer families a fairer choice between owning a home and renting one, and to ensure fairness between one citizen and another in giving and receiving help towards housing costs. As this policy is implemented, Government subsidies are available for local authorities which incur financial deficits in clearing slums and providing adequate public sector housing in areas of housing shortage. Another major objective is to enable more people with moderate means to become owner-occupiers. The Government is specially concerned to ensure that best use is made of the existing housing stock.

A national system of rent rebate and allowance schemes is being introduced to assist poorer tenants in both the public and private sectors. Operated by local authorities, the schemes are financed by central Government, where their cost results in a deficit for the authorities.

RESEARCH AND DEVELOPMENT

Within the Department of the Environment housing research is mostly carried out at the Building Research Establishment, which is the main centre for construction research, by the Housing Development Directorate, which concentrates on design and social policy research, and by the Economics and

Statistics Directorate. In Scotland central Government housing research is carried out by the Housing Research and Development Group of the Scottish Development Department. Many of the larger local authorities carry out their own housing research. There are also a number of multi-disciplinary centres at universities such as the Centre for Urban and Regional Studies at Birmingham, and the independent Centre for Environmental Studies, which have specialised in research related to housing. Another independent centre is the National Building Agency which is concerned chiefly with production and technical aspects. The Government is advised on the need for and application of research by the Construction and Housing Research Advisory Council.

PUBLIC SECTOR HOUSING
Public housing authorities in Britain own some 6 million houses and flats and in 1972 completed about 130,000 new dwellings—39 per cent of the total house construction in the country. The number of houses owned by each authority varies; some have less than 100, while, for example, the Birmingham City Council has nearly 150,000. Authorities plan their own building programmes within the framework of Government policy.

Finance
Local authorities in Great Britain normally meet the capital costs of new house construction by raising loans on the open market or by borrowing from the Public Works Loan Board. Current expenditure, including maintenance costs and loan interest and repayments, is met from rents, supplemented by subsidies from the Exchequer and sometimes (particularly in Scotland) from the rates.

Subsidies for public housing in 1972–73 totalled some £280 million in England and Wales and about £60 million in Scotland. In the past Government subsidies were designed to reduce the interest paid by all local authorities on loans raised to finance house building. These subsidies enabled many authorities to maintain rents below those current in the open market. However, under the Housing Finance Act 1972 and Housing (Financial Provisions) (Scotland) Act 1972, these have been replaced by new subsidies designed to concentrate assistance on those authorities and tenants in greatest need.

Under the Acts all local authorities in England and Wales are required to base their rents upon the 'fair rent' principle which already applies to much rented accommodation in the private sector (see p 77), while those in Scotland must ensure that rents are at such a level that (taking new subsidies into account) they can balance their housing expenditure without any deficit falling on the rates. In England and Wales the level of council house rents is intended to enable an increasing number of local authorities—especially those with a high proportion of older council housing—to meet their housing expenditure without further subsidies. Other authorities—those with substantial building programmes and a large proportion of newer council housing—will be in deficit and they will be assisted by new subsidies designed to help them balance expenditure. Similar subsidies will assist those authorities in Scotland which have rising expenditure resulting from a heavy building programme.

Supplementary subsidies have been made available under the Acts to assist local authorities throughout Great Britain with slum clearance. In addition, the Acts provide for the introduction of a national system of rent rebates covering all local authority tenants, and financed largely by Government subsidy where they cause a deficit in housing revenue accounts. The scheme will assist poorer tenants in meeting rents of accommodation suited to their needs.

In Northern Ireland, the capital expenditure of the Northern Ireland Housing Executive is financed by loans raised on the open market or borrowed from the Government Loans Fund. New dwellings completed by the executive qualify for Government subsidy at a rate which varies according to the number of persons for whom each dwelling is designed.

Tenants

In selecting tenants for new or vacant dwellings, local authorities normally give preference to large families and to those living in overcrowded or unsatisfactory conditions, but they are free to allocate houses according to their own schemes. Authorities normally establish waiting lists and treat applicants (outside priority categories) in order of application; some require applicants to fulfil residence requirements before they are accepted on waiting lists.

Construction and Design

Although a number of authorities employ direct labour which may, after competition, build houses, most building is undertaken by private firms under contract. Some authorities work in consortia to make the best use of industrialised systems in their housebuilding programmes.

Dwellings are constructed to meet the needs of different sizes of household. More than a quarter are of the single bedroom type suitable for smaller households including the elderly, but the majority are designed for families and have two or three bedrooms, two living rooms and a kitchen, bathroom and lavatory. The standard of new local authority housing has improved considerably in recent years, particularly in the floor space provided and heating systems installed. In England and Wales in 1971 over 92·4 per cent of new dwellings had central heating, and houses built for families of four or five people had a superficial area of 961 square feet (89 square metres) and cost an average of about £3,800 to build.

Housing for Elderly People

Special attention has been given to the provision of housing designed to meet the needs of old people. This broadly takes two forms. The more active old people are accommodated in self-contained bungalows and flats, which normally comprise a living-room, bedroom, kitchen, bathroom and lavatory; while for those who are not so active, flatlets are provided. Each flatlet for a single old person normally comprises a bed-sitting-room, kitchen and lavatory with a wash basin. Bathrooms are shared on the basis of not less than one to four flatlets. Flatlets for couples have a living-room and bedroom instead of a bed-sitting-room and their own bathroom. All new dwellings for old people are provided with central heating.

The flatlet type of accommodation is provided with the services of a resident warden whose job is to answer emergency calls from the tenants, calling in the domiciliary social services when necessary and providing assistance in a number of ways.

The dwellings themselves incorporate such features as windows which can be easily opened, cupboards, shelves and sinks at convenient heights and hand-holds in bathrooms and lavatories.

HOME OWNERSHIP

In 1972 over 200,000 private sector dwellings were completed in Britain, almost all of which were intended for owner-occupation. The number of people owning their own houses has more than doubled in the last 20 years, and the 10 million owner-occupied dwellings in Britain now account for half of the total housing stock. Although most owner-occupied houses were built for that purpose, many private rented dwellings have also been sold for owner-occupation. Local and new town authorities are encouraged by the Government to offer houses for sale to sitting tenants and sales are increasing. The Government also encourages voluntary housing societies which provide co-ownership housing (a form of tenure similar to owner-occupation).

Mortgage Loans

Loans to enable people to buy their own homes are available from various sources, including building societies, insurance companies, friendly societies and local authorities.

Building societies are the most important of these agencies. They do not build houses themselves but provide long-term loans on the security of property bought for owner-occupation. They normally advance 80 per cent of their valuation of a house but it is possible to borrow up to 95 per cent or in some cases 100 per cent. Loans are normally repayable over periods of 20 or 25 years (up to 30 or 35 years in exceptional circumstances) by equal monthly instalments to cover capital and interest. The average price of new houses mortgaged to building societies in 1972 was £7,398; houses in London and the south-east of England cost some 40 per cent more than the national average. In 1972 the societies advanced some £3,650 million.

Local authorities are encouraged to concentrate their mortgage resources on helping people with housing needs who are unable to obtain loans elsewhere. Their mortgage lending in 1972 amounted to £190 million.

Financial Assistance

Owner-occupiers are entitled to tax relief on their mortgage interest payments, and in 1972–73 this amounted to £390 million. An alternative form of assistance—the option mortgage scheme—designed to help those with smaller incomes was introduced in 1968. Under the scheme, borrowers receive, through the lending agency, a subsidy (instead of tax relief) which reduces the rate of mortgage interest which they pay by up to 3 per cent. Subsidy payments under the option mortgage scheme amounted in 1972–73 to £28 million. Associated with the scheme is the option mortgage guarantee scheme, whereby mortgage loans of up to 100 per cent of the valuation of a house (not exceeding £7,500) may be made to those participating. In Northern Ireland, the Government pays subsidies to private people who build dwellings for owner-occupation or letting.

Building Standards

For building in the private sector the National House Builders' Registration Council (NHBRC) sets standards and enforces them by inspection and certification. Almost all new private housing built for sale carries the NHBRC ten-year guarantee against any major structural defect. A two-year guarantee is also given against faulty workmanship. Most building societies do not grant mortgages on a new house unless it is covered by a NHBRC certificate.

PRIVATELY RENTED HOUSING

During the last 20 years there has been a steady decline in the number of rented dwellings available from private landlords—from nearly 45 per cent of the housing stock in 1951 to about 13 per cent in 1972. Major factors in this decline have been the increased demand for owner-occupation, the greater availability of public rented housing, and the operation of rent restriction. Privately rented dwellings form a high proportion of Britain's older housing and many have been demolished under slum clearance programmes. Of the nearly 3 million dwellings which remain, about three-quarters are 50 years old or more. While most landlords in Britain are private individuals with limited holdings, a proportion of all privately rented housing is provided by the small number of larger property owners, including property companies.

Most privately rented dwellings are subject to rent restriction under legislation which provides separate machinery for dealing with unfurnished and furnished accommodation. Tenants have a wide degree of security of tenure, and eviction from any dwelling (without a court order) and harassment of occupiers are criminal offences with severe penalties.

Unfurnished Accommodation

An estimated five-sixths of all private rented accommodation in Great Britain is let unfurnished. Unfurnished accommodation is usually subject to either 'rent control' or 'rent regulation'. In either case the tenants enjoy comprehensive rights to security of tenure. Rent control applies to some half of the unfurnished dwellings—those with a 1956 rateable value of £30 or less (£40 in London and Scotland). Where the tenancy has continued since July 1957 tenants of controlled dwellings pay fixed rents determined by reference to 1956 gross values or, in Scotland, to historic rent levels. These are very low by comparison with other rents. Landlords of controlled dwellings whose houses are of a satisfactory standard or who improve them to such a standard are able to transfer them to the alternative system of rent regulation. The transfer of all remaining controlled tenancies into the rent regulation system is being speeded up.

Rent regulation was introduced in 1965 and applies to almost all private unfurnished dwellings (but not while they remain controlled under previous legislation). Under the Housing Finance Act 1972, its principle has been extended to cover rented dwellings (within the rateable limits) owned by public housing authorities (see p 74) and housing associations and societies.

Under the rent regulation procedure, a 'fair rent' may be fixed for a tenancy by independent rent officers at the request of the landlord, the tenant, or both. Factors taken into account by rent officers in determining rents include the age, character and locality of the house. To eliminate any artificial value derived from scarcity, the assumption is made that for similar dwellings to let in the area demand does not exceed supply. If the landlord or tenant objects to the decision of the rent officer, the case is referred to a rent assessment committee. Since 1965 some 450,000 fair rents have been registered for the first time. Once determined, the rent is not normally reviewed for at least three years. Controlled and regulated tenants enjoy security of tenure.

The tenants of private unfurnished accommodation will be eligible for assistance with their rent under a national scheme of rent allowances to be introduced in January 1973. Operated by local authorities, the scheme is financed mainly by Government subsidies.

In Northern Ireland, houses of a 1939 rateable value of less than £50 are subject to rent control with rents fixed by reference to their rateable value in that year. However, prescribed increases were permitted in the rents of certain controlled dwellings in 1951 and 1956, and dwellings of which landlords are in, or obtain, possession and dwellings completed since 1956 are freed from rent control.

Furnished Accommodation

The tenants or landlords of furnished housing under the rateable value limits of the Rent Acts may refer tenancy agreements to a local rent tribunal for determination of a reasonable rent. Tribunals may grant tenants security of tenure for up to six months with a possibility of further periods if they so decide. Tenants in furnished accommodation are to be covered by a rent allowance scheme.

HOUSING ASSOCIATIONS AND SOCIETIES

Since the early 1960s the Government has done much to encourage the growth of non-profit-making housing associations and societies, which between them own some 200,000 dwellings in Great Britain; in 1972 they completed nearly 8,000 new dwellings.

Housing associations have long existed as voluntary bodies set up for the purpose of providing low-rent housing for people in need. The associations have in the past borrowed money to finance housebuilding, mainly from local authorities, who may make up to 100 per cent loans. Encouragement to purchase and convert old houses into new dwellings was offered by the Housing Acts of 1969 which provided for a 20-year subsidy equivalent to three-eighths of all charges (capital and interest) on loans raised for the purpose. Under the 1972 legislation housing associations will, like housing societies (see below), be able to borrow from the Housing Corporation for new building. The rents of housing association houses are to be based on fair-rent levels, and their tenants are to be entitled to rent allowances (see above). Where fair rents produce insufficient revenue to cover the initial cost of a scheme, associations receive a Government subsidy covering the deficit. The subsidy reduces, as rents increase, at intervals of three years.

Housing societies build dwellings either for co-ownership by a group of occupants or to let at unsubsidised rents. Following a pilot scheme introduced by the Housing Act 1961, the Housing Corporation was set up under the Housing Act 1964 to stimulate the formation of such societies. Half of the money needed for approved housing society schemes is advanced by building societies, with the Housing Corporation providing the remainder. Rented housing society dwellings like those owned by housing associations are being brought within the fair-rent and rent-allowance schemes.

IMPROVEMENT OF HOUSES

Private owners in Great Britain can obtain grants from local authorities to improve their houses by providing amenities such as baths and for carrying out other works to modernise their properties. Grants are also available for converting large houses or other buildings into flats. The grant normally amounts to half the approved cost of the works up to a grant limit of £1,000. If a house of three or more storeys is converted into flats the upper limit of grant is £1,200 for each flat provided. A Government contribution amounting to three-quarters of each grant is paid to the local authority. Aid on a similar basis is given by the Government to local authorities and housing associations, but this can include part of the cost of buying properties for conversions and improvement as well as that of carrying out works. Under the Housing Act 1971 increased grants up to a maximum of £1,500 (£1,800 in Scotland) are available for a limited period to private owners and local authorities within the development and intermediate areas, that is, areas with special economic problems.

Since improvement grants were first introduced in 1949, nearly 2 million dwellings in England and Wales and some 150,000 in Scotland have been improved with their aid. In 1972 grants were approved for some 368,000 dwellings in Great Britain—a 68 per cent increase over the previous year. Grants for house improvement are also provided in Northern Ireland.

In order to tackle systematically the improvement of whole areas of older housing, local authorities in England and Wales have been given powers to declare 'general improvement areas'. The aim in these areas is to encourage householders to improve their dwellings with the aid of grants, while the local authority uses its comprehensive powers to improve the environment. A Government contribution is available on half the local authority's expenditure on environmental improvements on costs of up to £200 a house. There are similar grants in Scotland for the improvement of residential areas.

The Government is also proposing to empower local authorities to declare 'housing action areas' for a limited period in places of housing stress. Among the new measures envisaged are preferential rates of improvement grant and new grants for repairs alone, powers to compel owners to improve their houses to a given standard and powers to ensure that housing associations would be given first refusal of a tenanted property offered for sale in the area.

SLUM CLEARANCE

Over 2·5 million people have been rehoused in England and Wales since the mid-1950s as a result of slum clearance programmes, and during 1972 nearly

90,000 houses were demolished or closed in Great Britain as a result of slum clearance action. Some housing authorities have eliminated all their slums and many others expect to achieve this within a very few years. Local authorities now receive special financial assistance from the Government if they incur a loss on slum clearance operations. The house-building programmes of some authorities have increased considerably and in many cases the designation of new towns nearby has further eased their housing problems.

Housing authorities must see that accommodation is available for people displaced by slum clearance. Owners of land compulsorily acquired during clearance programmes receive as compensation either the full market value or, if the land consists of unfit houses, a sum based on the value of the cleared site. Additional payments are made to most owner-occupiers of unfit houses to bring their compensation up to market value.

NEW TOWNS

The New Towns Act 1946 and corresponding legislation for Scotland and Northern Ireland gives the Secretary of State for the Environment in England and the Secretaries of State for Scotland, Wales and Northern Ireland power to designate any area of land as the site of a new town. A development corporation (development commission in Northern Ireland) plans the development of each town. Several substantially completed new towns in England have become the responsibility of the Commission for the New Towns, a Government-appointed agency. The new towns help to ease overcrowding in large cities by providing homes and employment in new areas planned in advance with full services and amenities within convenient distance of every inhabitant.

The 33 new towns designated in Britain—23 in England and Wales, 6 in Scotland and 4 in Northern Ireland—contain over 1·7 million people.

The capital cost to corporations of developing the new towns in Great Britain is financed from public funds and is repayable over 60 years from the date of borrowing.

The transfer of population from congested industrial cities to other areas suitable for expansion, where employment is provided, has also taken place under the Town Development Act 1952 and the Housing and Town Development (Scotland) Act 1957. The cities make bilateral agreements with small towns wishing to expand, and help to provide the homes and other buildings required. Both authorities contribute to the cost. Schemes in England and Wales are providing some 163,000 homes in this way.

LEGAL AID AND ADVICE

BRITAIN'S legal aid scheme helps people of limited means and resources to meet the cost of all work normally done by a lawyer. People who receive aid under the scheme may be required to pay a contribution, but otherwise lawyers' costs and expenses are paid out of a state legal aid fund drawn from three sources: contributions from assisted people, costs recovered from opposite parties in litigation, and a grant from the Exchequer. There are some financial limits on the amount of work a lawyer can do for a client under the scheme, but these do not generally apply where court proceedings—civil or criminal—are concerned.

Legal Aid in Civil Proceedings

Free legal aid is available to people whose disposable income does not exceed £300 a year, and whose disposable capital is £250 or less, and contributory legal aid to those whose disposable income does not exceed £950 a year and whose disposable capital is less than £1,200 or such larger figure as may be prescribed.[1] An assisted person is liable for a maximum contribution towards the cost of his case of a third of the sum by which his disposable capital exceeds £250 a year, together with the amount by which his disposable capital exceeds £125 or such larger figure as may be prescribed.

The legal aid scheme in England and Wales is run by the Law Society (the professional organisation of solicitors) under the general guidance of the Lord Chancellor. It is operated by 14 area committees and a network of local committees, composed of barristers and solicitors (who may be paid a moderate fee), with a salaried staff.

An applicant for legal aid must first approach the appropriate local committee or, in the case of legal aid for an appeal, the area committee, and show that he has reasonable grounds for asserting or disputing a claim. If his application is successful, he is entitled to select from a panel a solicitor (who, if necessary, instructs a barrister), and the case is then conducted in the ordinary way, except that no money passes between the assisted person and his solicitor—payments being made in and out of the legal aid fund. The costs of an action which an assisted litigant loses against an unassisted opponent may also, in cases of severe financial hardship and if the court so orders, be met out of the fund. Local and area committees have the right to refuse assistance if it appears unreasonable that the applicant should receive it in the particular circumstances of a case; both solicitors and barristers have a duty to review the case at each stage to see that it is not being pursued unreasonably at the public expense. Legal aid is not available for proceedings in tribunals (except the Lands Tribunal and the Commons Commissioners), coroners' courts and cases where redress is sought for alleged defamation. The net cost to public funds of legal aid in civil cases in England and Wales in 1971–72 was more than £7·5 million.

---

[1] Assessment of disposable income and capital are made by the Supplementary Benefits Commission and are governed by regulations which allow for deductions from gross income for maintenance of dependants, interest on loans, income tax, rent and other matters for which a person may reasonably provide out of income, and deductions for the value of a person's house, furniture and other household effects from his capital.

In Scotland the legal aid scheme is administered by the Law Society of Scotland through a supervisory central committee, the Supreme Court Committee, and 16 local committees. To obtain legal aid in civil proceedings, an applicant must have a 'probable cause' of action—that is, reasonable grounds for taking, defending or being party to the legal proceedings in view. Assistance is available in connection with appeals to the House of Lords from the Court of Session, in civil proceedings before the Court of Session, the Lands Valuation Appeal Court, the Scottish Land Court, the Lands Tribunal for Scotland and the sheriff courts, and in matters not involving litigation. Where no litigation is involved, the applicant must show that he has reasonable grounds for taking the proposed legal action.

In Northern Ireland the legal aid scheme is administered by the Incorporated Law Society of Northern Ireland under the general guidance of the Department of Home Affairs. The scheme provides for legal aid in proceedings in the Supreme Court, the county courts and in certain civil proceedings in magistrates' courts.

Legal Aid in Criminal Proceedings

In criminal proceedings in England and Wales a legal aid order may be made by the court or courts concerned if it appears that a defendant's means are such that he requires financial help in meeting the costs of the proceedings in which he is involved. An order must be made when a person is committed for trial on a charge of murder or applies for leave to appeal from the Court of Appeal (Criminal Division) to the House of Lords. No person can be sentenced for the first time to a term of imprisonment, borstal training or detention in a detention centre unless he is legally represented, or has been refused, or has failed to apply for, legal aid after having been informed of his right to do so. No limit of income or capital above which a person is ineligible for legal aid is specified, but the court has power to order applicants to pay a reasonable contribution towards the cost of the case according to their means.

Legal aid in criminal proceedings may consist of representation by a solicitor and counsel assigned by the court, but in most proceedings in magistrates' courts the recipient is entitled only to the services of a solicitor, and in Crown Court proceedings the court may, in cases of urgency (when there is no time to instruct a solicitor), order that legal aid shall consist of representation by counsel only. A solicitor may appear in, conduct and address the court in criminal proceedings in the Crown Court on appeal from a magistrates' court or on committal of a person to be sentenced or dealt with if he (or any solicitor in his employment or by whom he is employed) appeared on behalf of the defendant in the magistrates' court.

In appeal cases before the Crown Court legal aid may be granted by a magistrates' court or the Crown Court. The granting of legal aid for appeals to the Court of Appeal (Criminal Division) rests with that court, which may also grant legal aid for the purpose of a further appeal to the House of Lords.

The cost of legal aid in magistrates' courts is paid out of the legal aid fund. In the higher courts payments are borne by the central Government.

Legal aid in Scottish criminal proceedings is available to all people in custody on their first appearance in the sheriff courts. Otherwise, it is granted for proceedings in these courts and in the High Court of Justiciary at the discretion of the courts themselves, except in appeals, when the final decision whether or not it should be granted is in the hands of the Supreme Court Committee of the Law Society of Scotland.

In Northern Ireland free legal aid is available in trials on indictment before courts of assize and in county courts, and in criminal proceedings before magistrates' courts. It is also available for appeals from magistrates' courts to the county court and in appeals from county courts and courts of assize to the Court of Appeal (Criminal Division).

Legal Advice and Assistance

Under new provisions for legal advice and assistance, introduced in Great Britain in April 1973, a person may obtain help on any matter normally within a solicitor's practice, except for taking steps in court proceedings (for these legal aid is available in the ways outlined above, although magistrates' courts and county courts have power to appoint a solicitor to represent a person appearing before them). This help includes giving advice, writing letters, drafting wills, obtaining opinions from a barrister and visiting a police station or prison. A solicitor may act for a client until his costs and expenses reach a total of £25 (although, if necessary, authority may be obtained from the Law Society for this limit to be exceeded). A person seeking help has to give the solicitor brief details about his income and savings to show that he comes within the financial limits allowed by the scheme. People with disposable capital of up to £250 who are also receiving either supplementary benefits (see p 18) or family income supplement (see p 12) are within the financial limits; other people are also eligible provided their disposable capital does not exceed £250 and their weekly disposable income does not exceed £20 (in this case a small contribution may be payable).

Similar provisions are proposed for Northern Ireland.

TREATMENT OF OFFENDERS[1]

THE CHIEF AIMS of the penal systems of Britain are to deter the potential law-breaker and to reform the convicted offender. The element of deterrence is intended to lie in the fear of detection, public trial and possibility of punishment rather than in the severity of the punishment itself. In England and Wales the Home Secretary is assisted by an Advisory Council on the Penal System, which makes recommendations on specific aspects of the prevention of crime and the treatment of offenders. The Scottish Council on Crime keeps under review questions relating to the prevention of crime and the treatment of offenders in Scotland, in consultation with the Secretary of State for Scotland.

PENALTIES

Methods current in British penal practice include imprisonment and, for certain categories of young offender, other forms of custodial treatment (thes emay include training at a borstal, at an attendance centre, in a detention centre or in a remand home, approved school or community centre—details are given on pp 41–43). In addition an offender may be put on probation; fined; ordered to pay compensation; given an absolute or (in England, Wales and Northern Ireland) conditional discharge for up to three years, or 'bound over'—that is to say, required to pledge money, with or without sureties, 'to keep the peace and be of good behaviour'. In England, Wales and Northern Ireland, if sentenced to imprisonment for two years or less, an offender may be given a suspended sentence, which means that the sentence will not actually be served unless he commits a further offence punishable with imprisonment within two years. If, however, he does commit such an offence the suspended sentence will normally take effect and a further sentence may be imposed. In addition, under the Criminal Justice Act 1972, the courts have been given the power to order an offender, made subject to a suspended sentence of more than six months' imprisonment, to be placed under the supervision of a probation officer. (Other new penalty provisions introduced by the Act are outlined on p 85.)

The mandatory penalty for murder in Britain—the death penalty has been abolished—is imprisonment for life, a sentence which may also be imposed for manslaughter and certain other offences, including rape, robbery with violence, and arson.

Except in cases of murder, for which the penalty is prescribed by law, the court which tries the offender has discretion to select the penalty that it considers most suitable in the light of the nature and gravity of the offence and the information available about the character and needs of the offender. In certain cases this discretion is modified by statutory provisions designed for the most part to ensure that prison sentences are kept to a minimum. In England and Wales, no offender under the age of 17 may be sentenced to

---

[1]Details of provisions affecting children in trouble are given on pp 41–43. For fuller information on this subject generally, see COI reference pamphlet *The Treatment of Offenders in Britain*, R4414.

imprisonment; for those aged 17 and under 21 prison sentences must be for less than six months or for more than three years (except that persistent offenders may be sent to prison for 18 months or more). In Scotland no offender under 21 may be sent to prison; in cases involving people aged 16 and under 21 years, where neither borstal training nor detention in a detention centre is thought appropriate, detention in a young offenders' institution may be ordered. (For special sentences for young offenders, see pp 41–43).

The Criminal Justice Act 1972 provides for the introduction of a number of new penalties, the modification of some existing penalties and the making of a number of other changes to the penal system and the administration of justice. The new penalties include community service orders (which may require an offender to perform up to 240 hours of unpaid work of benefit to the community in his spare time), criminal bankruptcy orders (which provide the basis of bankruptcy proceedings against certain offenders convicted of major crimes against property), the forfeiture by the offender of property used or intended for use for the purposes of crime, and the disqualification from driving of a person using a vehicle for the commission of a crime. In addition it is now possible for courts to attach a condition to a probation order requiring an offender to attend for up to 60 days at a day training centre. Among existing penalties modified under the Act are those concerning reparation by the offender and suspended sentences. In connection with the latter, the Act removes the restriction requiring courts to suspend sentences of not more than six months. The Act also provides that, in certain circumstances, courts have the power to defer passing sentences on an offender for up to six months.

ADMINISTRATIVE AUTHORITIES

In England and Wales the Home Secretary is the Minister generally responsible for legislation relating to the treatment of offenders, for collecting statistical and other information about the operation of the penal system, for keeping penal methods under review, and for bringing information about these methods to the attention of the courts. He has specific responsibilities for promoting the efficiency of the probation service, and for providing, maintaining and managing prisons, borstal institutions, detention centres, remand centres and attendance centres (see p 41). Prison policy is carried out by the Prison Department of the Home Office through the agency of the prison service which operates under a director-general and includes a headquarters organisation, regional directors, the governors and staff of the penal establishments and members of particular professions, such as medical officers, chaplains and social workers.

Reports to the Home Secretary on the administration of institutions in the penal system are made by boards of visitors appointed by the Home Secretary, not less than two members of which must be justices of the peace. The other functions of these bodies include acting as the superior disciplinary authority for reports of a more serious nature against prisoners and providing an independent channel of complaint for any prisoner having a grievance.

The boards of visitors also advise on the release on licence of the inmates of borstals. The work of the boards helps to preserve local interest, and is voluntary.

The penal systems in Scotland and Northern Ireland are based on principles similar to those applied in England and Wales. In Scotland the system is the responsibility of the Secretary of State for Scotland, and in Northern Ireland of the Department of Home Affairs.

PRISONS

The aims of the prison service are briefly to provide for the detention of those committed to custody under the law in conditions generally acceptable to society and to develop methods of treatment and training which will 'encourage and assist them to lead a good and useful life'.[1] To this end prisoners are classified into groups, according to their record, character, potentialities and the risk they present to security, and assigned, so far as circumstances permit, to the establishment best suited to their needs. Untried prisoners are separated from convicted prisoners and, as far as practicable, those under 21 are separated from those over that age.

Prisons to which offenders may be committed directly by a court are known as 'local prisons'; all are closed establishments. Other prisons, which may be open or closed, receive prisoners on transfer from local prisons. To relieve overcrowding in local prisons and generally to improve prisoners' conditions, new prisons are being built and existing establishments redeveloped and modernised. During the last ten years the accommodation available in England and Wales has been increased by 9,500 places, and the current building programme envisages an additional 11,500 places by 1975–76. In Scotland 1,500 new places have been provided, and a further 3,000 places will be made available by the early 1980s.

Remission of Sentence and Parole

On reception under sentence, all prisoners, except those sentenced to imprisonment for life, are credited with remission of one-third of their sentence provided that this does not reduce their sentence below 31 days (in Scotland, 30 days). In addition, except in Northern Ireland, prisoners serving fixed sentences become eligible for consideration for release on parole after serving one-third of their sentence, subject to a minimum of one year. Each eligible prisoner is first considered by a local review committee which reports to the Home Secretary or the Secretary of State for Scotland on his suitability for parole. The Minister concerned has power in some cases to grant or refuse parole, while others he refers to the Parole Board for England and Wales or the Parole Board for Scotland, each of which consists of a chairman and a number of other members, appointed by the Home Secretary and the Secretary of State for Scotland respectively. Where the Parole Board recommends favourably, the decision whether or not to release the prisoner depends finally on the Minister, but where the Board does not recommend release the Minister has no power to grant parole.[2] The licence remains in force until the

---

[1] Rule 1 of the Prison Rules made by the Home Secretary for prisons in England and Wales.
[2] Under the Criminal Justice Act 1972 the Home Secretary has the power, in certain classes of case, to release a person on licence on the recommendation of the local review committee.

date on which the prisoner would have been released if he had not been licensed or, for prisoners serving extended sentences (in England and Wales only) and offenders sentenced while under 21 years of age, until the end of the sentence.

Prisoners serving life sentences are also eligible for release on licence. In Great Britain the usual practice in such cases is to seek the views of the local review committee after the offender has served seven years. Each case is considered by the Home Secretary or Secretary of State for Scotland and forwarded to the Parole Board concerned. The Lord Chief Justice in England or the Lord Justice General in Scotland (as the case may be) and, if he is available, the judge who presided at the trial must, by law, be consulted before any life sentence prisoner is released. In Northern Ireland, where the Department for Home Affairs is responsible for the release on licence of prisoners serving life sentences, the judiciary is similarly consulted.

Employment

In England and Wales prison work is controlled by the Directorate of Industries and Supply of the Prison Department of the Home Office, which comprises administrative, executive, professional and technical staff. Technical advice and services to workshops are provided by visits from regional and headquarters staff. Industrial managers at establishments assist governors with the day-to-day running of the workshops. Farms and gardens attached to penal establishments are controlled by the Chief Farms and Gardens Officer at the Directorate's headquarters. In Scotland industries and supplies are controlled by a branch of the Prisons Division of the Scottish Home and Health Department. In Northern Ireland general supervision of prison work is exercised by the Department of Home Affairs. The main aim of all prison industries is to give inmates training and experience to help them obtain and keep employment on discharge.

The primary source of work for prison inmates lies in the requirements of the prison service itself, that is to say, building and maintenance, domestic services and equipment. Goods and services are also supplied to other Government departments and, on an increasing scale, to other purchasers, both inside and outside the public service. A few prisoners are employed outside prison in agriculture and on work such as archaeological excavation and the preservation of canals.

In England, Wales and Scotland, small payments are made to inmates for the work they do; in some prisons payments above the minimum are made on the basis of output and skill; in Northern Ireland a progressive system of earnings, related to work done, is being gradually introduced.

Any prisoner serving a sentence of four years or more may be considered for employment in an ordinary civilian job outside prison for about six months before his discharge. Prisoners selected for the scheme may live either in prison or in a prison hostel; they are paid normal wages, from which they support their families and meet their own expenses.

Education

Education for those in custody in Great Britain is provided by local education authorities. In England and Wales, where arrangements are being developed under a Chief Education Officer, there is close liaison with the Department of Education and Science, and in Scotland with the Scottish Education Department. Most prisons have an education officer assisted by a number of part-time teachers and, usually, one or more full-time teachers. Prisoners may attend evening classes and take correspondence courses when these are available and other educational facilities, such as physical training, concerts, plays, films, lectures and group discussions, are arranged where facilities allow; prisoners may also use the prison libraries, which depend largely upon the local public libraries for their stocks. For selected prisoners vocational training courses, leading to an acknowledged qualification, such as that of the City and Guilds of London Institute, are provided, and experiments with Open University studies and full-time education are being undertaken. Education in prisons in Northern Ireland is the responsibility of the Department of Home Affairs. Facilities similar to those in Great Britain are provided under the direction of the Prison Service Education Officer.

Medical Services

Medical attention is provided by full-time and part-time medical officers whose duties include the care of the physical and mental health of prison inmates, and the oversight of those services which affect health in prisons.

In a few prisons there are large, fully equipped hospitals where major surgery can be undertaken and treatment by visiting specialists given both to inmates and to prisoners from other establishments. There is also one psychiatric prison (in England and Wales) for some 350 people.

Several prisons have their own psychiatric clinics, to which prisoners from other establishments may be referred and, in England and Wales, there is a prison psychological service, whose officers assist governors and medical officers in their work of examining and classifying prisoners. The hospital facilities of the National Health Service are available for the treatment of prisoners in appropriate cases and arrangements may be made, where necessary, for prisoners to receive treatment after release.

Privileges and Discipline

All prisoners, from the beginning of their sentence, have a legal right to write and receive letters and to be visited by their relations at regular intervals. They also have such privileges as additional letters and visits, the use of books, periodicals and newspapers, and the right to make purchases from the canteen with money they have earned in prison. Depending on the facilities available at individual establishments, they may be granted the further privileges of dining and recreation in association and watching television in the evening.

Breaches of discipline are dealt with by the prison governor, or board of visitors, who have power to order, among other penalties, forfeiture of remission and forfeiture of privileges.

WELFARE AND AFTER-CARE

Welfare in prisons is the general concern of the prison staff as a whole, and in particular of the chaplains and assistant governors, but special responsibilities attach to prison welfare officers, who, in England, Wales and Northern Ireland, are probation officers seconded by the probation and after-care service. (In Scotland, prison welfare officers are specially appointed for this purpose.) The functions of these officers include helping the prisoner in his relationships with individuals and organisations outside the prison, and making plans for the prisoner's after-care, working closely in this connection with colleagues in the probation and after-care service and with other agencies in the community, including voluntary bodies, whose help the prisoner or his family may need either during sentence or after release.

For the spiritual welfare of the inmates, a chaplain of the Church of England (in Scotland of the Church of Scotland, and in Northern Ireland of the Church of Ireland and of the Presbyterian Church), a Roman Catholic priest and a minister of the Methodist Church are appointed to every prison. Ministers of other denominations are either appointed or specially called in as required. Chaplains not only hold regular services, but also visit every prisoner soon after reception, shortly before release and regularly during sentence, and pay daily visits to all prisoners who are sick or confined to their cells and to any others who apply to see them.

Prisoners may also receive visits from specially appointed prison visitors, whose work is voluntary and in England and Wales is co-ordinated and guided by the National Association of Prison Visitors.

In England and Wales pre-release courses are conducted at all prisons. During these courses experts hold open forum with prisoners nearing their release on the domestic, social and employment problems with which they are likely to be faced. Certain categories of prisoners may be granted home leave towards the end of their sentences to enable them to preserve links with their families and friends, or to make new contacts with people, including potential employers, who may be able to assist them on release. Some categories are considered for two periods of home leave, one allowing five clear days and the other a week-end at home, and others for one period of five days at home.

Offenders released on licence are subject to statutory supervision after release by probation officers of the probation and after-care service, to which offenders not subject to compulsory supervision may also apply for help. Those who fail to observe the conditions of statutory supervision are liable to have their licences revoked. The Probation and After-Care Service is assisted by a number of voluntary organisations which are particularly concerned with providing accommodation for ex-offenders.

In Northern Ireland after-care duties are likewise carried out by probation and after-care officers; in Scotland responsibility for statutory and voluntary after-care is vested in social workers from the local authority social work departments.

PROBATION

Probation is designed to secure the rehabilitation of an offender while he remains at work or at school under the supervision of a probation officer, whose duty it is to advise, assist and befriend him. A cardinal feature of the service is that it relies on the co-operation of the offender. Before making a probation order, the court must explain its effects and make sure that the probationer understands that if he fails to comply with the requirements of the order he will be liable to be dealt with for the original offence. A probation order can be made only if the offender is 17 years of age or over and must have his consent; it usually requires the probationer to keep in regular touch with the probation officer, to be of good behaviour and to lead an industrious life. It may also require him to live in a specified place, to submit to treatment for his mental condition, or, where appropriate arrangements exist, to attend a day training centre for up to 60 days. A probation order is made for not less than one year and not more than three years.

In England, Wales and Northern Ireland, the services of probation officers are available to every criminal court. In England and Wales their appointment is the responsibility of probation and after-care committees, composed for the most part of justices—first appointments, except in the case of professionally trained officers, being subject to confirmation by the Home Secretary. In Northern Ireland the Department of Home Affairs appoints probation officers. The promotion and recognition of courses for the training of social workers in Britain, including probation officers, is the responsibility of the Central Council for the Education and Training of Social Workers.

In Scotland, where there is no separate probation service, the local authority social work departments provide the services and officers required by the criminal courts in their areas. Offenders subject to probation orders or to after-care supervision following release from a penal institution are supervised by specially approved social workers from these departments. Recruitment is the responsibility of the local authority concerned, and appointments are not subject to ministerial confirmation. Unqualified staff appointed to posts in social work departments can be seconded for professional training after one year in post.

VOLUNTARY ORGANISATIONS

VOLUNTARY ORGANISATIONS have been a feature of life in Britain for centuries and most social reform owes its origin to groups of like-minded people who combined their resources to improve the life of the community. The growth of voluntary organisations, particularly in the second half of the nineteenth century, was followed by further development in the early part of the twentieth century, accompanying the advance of government functions in the field of social welfare. During the second world war and in the years immediately afterwards when a comprehensive system of social security was being evolved an even greater number of voluntary organisations came into being. Now that the State has assumed much wider responsibility for the social services, voluntary action works in close partnership in many fields of activity. State services often work through voluntary societies, and statutory bodies and voluntary organisations co-operate closely.

Although many voluntary societies were, and a few still are, entirely administered by unpaid officials, the majority are now staffed by salaried administrators, and those concerned with personal services or casework employ trained social workers; but there are still large numbers of people from all walks of life who give part- and full-time unpaid service. An increasing number of organisations arrange training schemes for staff. A national centre for voluntary work, known as the Volunteer Centre, was set up in 1973 with an initial focus on the health and social services. The centre will collect and distribute information about recruitment, preparation and use of volunteers, encourage schemes for briefing and training, and promote study of how volunteers can be more widely and constructively used.

The National Council of Social Service is a representative body developing co-operation between voluntary societies and statutory authorities through consultation and joint action. It provides information, carries out research, initiates experiments and undertakes promotional work in Britain and overseas. The Scottish Council of Social Service, the Northern Ireland Council of Social Service and the Council of Social Service for Wales and Monmouthshire provide similar services.

The number of voluntary organisations now runs into thousands, ranging from large national societies to small local groups. Some are directly concerned with giving personal service, others with influencing public opinion. Some started as self-help organisations by groups seeking a solution to a common problem. The work of some is religious in inspiration, including such national organisations as the Salvation Army, the Young Men's Christian Association, the Young Women's Christian Association, the Society of Friends, the Crusade of Rescue and the Jewish Welfare Board. On a local scale, many of the good neighbour schemes which give help to the elderly, the sick and disabled are conducted by churches of many denominations, often now in co-operation with each other.

The Charity Commission

The Charity Commission, a Government department, maintains central and local registers of charities, which are open to public inspection, and gives free advice to trustees of charities. It makes schemes to modify their purposes or facilitate their administration, provides an officially guaranteed custodian trustee, and is closely concerned with The Charities Official Investment Fund, a common investment fund open to charities in England and Wales. It works to promote co-operation between charities and state services and encourages the institution of reviews of charities by local government authorities. The commissioners have powers to investigate the affairs of most charities.

Financing the Voluntary Services

Although voluntary organisations derive at least part of their funds from voluntary sources, central and local government are giving increasing financial aid, and legislation concerned with the social services makes provision for local authorities to support voluntary action in many fields. The voluntary contributions include subscriptions and donations from individuals and organisations, including industrial and commercial firms; and large charitable trusts, most of which were founded in the last 50 years, are an important source of income, especially for experimental and research work. Among the more important are the Calouste Gulbenkian Foundation, the Carnegie United Kingdom Trust, King George's Jubilee Trust, the National Corporation for the Care of Old People, the Nuffield Foundation, the Joseph Rowntree Charitable Trust, the Pilgrim Trust and the Wolfson Foundation.

Citizens' Advice Bureaux

A link between the individual and the services available to him is provided by Citizens' Advice Bureaux. This movement was started in 1939 as a war-time advice and information service and has developed into one of the largest voluntary undertakings in Britain. There are now some 540 bureaux dealing with over 1·5 million inquiries annually, and experience has shown that many people prefer to seek help from an independent rather than an official service. The bureaux interpret the law for those who have difficulty in understanding it and help the citizen to benefit from and use the services available to him. The National Citizens' Advice Bureau Council receives a Government grant and the majority of bureaux are supported by their respective local authorities.

Community Organisation

In communities of all sizes groups and individuals combine their experience and resources to meet specific needs and improve the quality of community life. In villages this may be by means of the parish council or village hall committee; in urban neighbourhoods through a community association; and in cities and counties by means of councils of social service and rural community councils.

The protection of the countryside and of buildings of architectural and historical interest is the concern of a growing number of national and local associations whose aim is to conserve and improve Britain's amenities.

Family Welfare Services

Some of the work done by voluntary bodies in providing help for families is described in the sections of this pamphlet dealing with health and personal social services. This includes family planning (see p 30), day care of children (see p 37), and help for children deprived of a normal home life (see p 38). In addition to these family welfare organisations there are some 165 marriage guidance councils in Britain, co-ordinated in England, Wales and Northern Ireland by the National Marriage Guidance Council, and in Scotland by the Scottish Marriage Guidance Council. The Catholic Marriage Advisory Council has some 54 local centres in England and Wales. Through these bodies free advice is given by voluntary counsellors to couples who are meeting problems in their married life and to young people approaching marriage. The Government makes grants for marriage guidance work to the headquarters of the national bodies, and local authorities may make grants to local marriage guidance councils.

Services for the Sick and Handicapped

A very large range of activities for the sick and handicapped both in the home and in clubs, residential homes and clinics are undertaken by voluntary workers. Voluntary service is given by the British Red Cross Society, the St John Ambulance Association and Brigade and the St Andrew's Scottish Ambulance Service, and a number of societies exist to help sufferers from particular disabilities, such as the Royal National Institute for the Blind, the Royal National Institute for the Deaf, The Spastics Society, the constituent members of the Central Council for the Disabled and their Scottish equivalents.

The majority of hospitals in England and Wales have their own Leagues of Friends or similar bodies of voluntary workers who organise and undertake a variety of services. Many hospitals also receive help from the British Red Cross Society, the Order of St John, the Women's Royal Voluntary Service, or other organisations. The operation of canteens for out-patients, and trolley-shops and library services for in-patients, escorting new patients, and visiting patients in the wards and at home when they have left hospital are among the tasks commonly undertaken.

The education of children who are blind, deaf or otherwise handicapped is undertaken by local authorities through the agency of special schools. The social work service for handicapped children and their families (see p 35) is provided either directly by the local authorities or sometimes by a voluntary organisation acting as their agents. Voluntary agencies, such as the National Society for Mentally Handicapped Children and the National Deaf Children's Society, also do much for handicapped children in their own homes.

Many voluntary associations, such as the Royal British Legion and other ex-Service organisations, give financial aid and personal service to disabled ex-Service men and women and their families. These bodies work in co-operation with the Department of Health and Social Security. The Disabled Living Foundation undertakes research, development and education concerning aids for disabled people and runs a permanent exhibition of equipment and a demonstration garden for the handicapped.

Mentally handicapped people are the responsibility of public authorities; but the voluntary bodies concerned with mental health have formed the

National Association for Mental Health, which carries out a wide programme of advisory, educational and therapeutic work.

A wide range of voluntary personal service is given by the Women's Royal Voluntary Service, which helps in every kind of practical difficulty, brings 'meals on wheels' to housebound invalids and old people, provides flatlets and clubs for the elderly, helps with family problems and assists in hospitals and clinics, as well as doing relief work in emergencies.

Youth Services

The part played by voluntary effort in partnership with local and central government in the provision of youth services together with activities in which service to the community is given by youth are described on pp 62–64.

Services for the Elderly

Most voluntary work done for elderly people is co-ordinated by old people's welfare committees which have been established in some 1,540 areas and are affiliated to Age Concern (the National Old People's Welfare Council). In Wales, Scotland and Northern Ireland there are also national councils which co-ordinate the work of local committees. The National Corporation for the Care of Old People, established by the Nuffield Foundation, stimulates and undertakes research into the welfare of the elderly. Some 3,000 homes for old and disabled people, run by voluntary bodies or privately, are registered with local authorities in Great Britain. In Northern Ireland voluntary homes are registered with the Department of Health and Social Services and private homes with the welfare authorities.

Citizens' Rights Groups

A number of organisations exist whose purpose is to provide advice and assistance to people unsure of their rights. One of the largest is the National Council for Civil Liberties (NCCL), which is an independent voluntary organisation formed to protect individual civil liberties and the rights of political, religious, racial and other minorities in Britain. The NCCL has groups in many cities. Specific purpose organisations such as the Child Poverty Action Group, or Release (which specialises in drugs cases) provide advice, usually free, to those with particular problems. Other organisations deal more generally with the interests of the public, for example, the Consumers' Association. Increasingly citizens' rights groups are developing on a community basis. The Claimants' Unions, for example, help people claim welfare benefits while a number of neighbourhood law centres have been established in London to dispense free legal advice. The emphasis with most of these groups is on informality and accessibility and many use shops or market stalls as centres from which to provide their services.

SPECIAL AREA SCHEMES

THE URBAN AID PROGRAMME

A four-year urban aid programme providing for Government-aided local authority expenditure of some £20 million to £25 million was launched at the end of 1968 to assist areas of special social need, in particular to relieve problems resulting from overcrowding, inadequate housing and schools, and other forms of deprivation. In 1970 the programme was extended to 1976 with total expenditure for the period 1968–76 of £60 million to £65 million. Up to October 1973 there had been nine phases of expenditure on the programme involving a total sum of £34 million approved for social service projects in urban areas of multiple deprivation throughout Great Britain—of which over £8·3 million was allocated for nursery education in England and Wales. Nursery education now forms part of the main programmes of the central education departments (see p 48). Projects are aided by a 75 per cent Government grant towards the capital costs and, in most cases, towards the first five years' running costs.

The urban aid programme is sponsored in England by the Home Office (which is also responsible for co-ordination), the Department of Education and Science, the Department of Health and Social Security and the Department of the Environment. The Scottish urban aid programme is administered by the Secretary of State for Scotland and the Welsh programme by the Secretary of State for Wales.

Projects approved include help for playgroups and the provision and improvement of nursery schools and classes (by December 1972, over 24,000 additional places in nursery schools and classes had been approved), day nurseries and playgrounds, language classes for immigrants, in-service training courses for teachers, children's homes, family advice centres, housing aid services, family planning clinics, help for community centres and summer holiday schemes for deprived children.

The urban aid programme involves current as well as capital expenditure. Local authorities are helped to make grants to a wide variety of voluntary organisations and activities including both local councils of social service and more specialised bodies like community relations councils, workshops for the elderly, local branches of the National Society for the Prevention of Cruelty to Children, the Family Planning Association, the Salvation Army, the Samaritans and many youth clubs and playgroups.

EDUCATIONAL PRIORITY AREAS

Discrimination in the allocation of resources in favour of 'educational priority areas' (EPAs) was recommended in 1967 by the Plowden Report on Children and their Primary Schools (see Reading List, p 115) as a way of improving the educational experience of children from poor homes in deprived areas. Since publication of the report, action to implement its recommendations has been taken in a number of ways including the urban programme, the community development project (see p 96) and a research project sponsored by the Department of Education and Science and the Social Science Research

Council. In addition the Government has taken direct action to improve the educational environment in deprived areas (there has been no official designation of educational priority areas), for example, by a special allocation of funds for school building and by introducing a £75 a year salary addition (now £105) for teachers employed in schools of exceptional difficulty. Local authorities have responded to the concept of the EPA, some of them by designating schools within their own areas as EPA schools, thus entitling them to additional allowances for books and equipment, others by the provision of special facilities such as 'opportunity' classes and adventure playgrounds. Some of the additional expenditure is being assisted under the urban aid programme with its favourable rate of grant.

In December 1972 the Government announced a ten-year expansion programme for education which has, as one of its main objectives, the provision of free nursery education to those children aged three and four whose parents wish them to benefit from it. As a consequence no new nursery education projects will be included under the urban aid programme but other types of educational projects which will be considered for approval include schemes to create links between the school and the family by the provision of extra staff such as EPA organisers, educational visitors and home/school liaison teachers.

COMMUNITY DEVELOPMENT PROJECT

The aim of the Community Development Project, which is a national action-research experiment carried out in selected urban localities, is to discover how far the problems experienced by people in a local community can be better understood and resolved through closer co-ordination of all the agencies involved—central and local government and the voluntary organisations—together with the local people themselves.

The Community Development Project began operating in 1970 in Coventry, Liverpool, Southwark and Glamorgan. In March 1971 extensions of the project to three new areas were announced—the West Riding of Yorkshire, the London Borough of Newham and the burgh of Paisley in Scotland. The county of Cumberland and the city of Newcastle upon Tyne were included in the project in August 1971 and in December of the same year it was announced that the project was being extended to a further three areas—the City of Birmingham, and the county boroughs of Oldham and Tynemouth. This brought the number of areas covered by the project in Great Britain to the planned total of 12. The action side of the project attracts a 75 per cent Government grant, and the research is wholly funded by central Government funds. The expenditure on social action in each community is estimated to reach its annual limit of £40,000 in the third and subsequent years of the experiment.

The procedure, once an area has been selected, is for an action team to be appointed to the local authority's staff and a complementary research and evaluation team formed from within a university or polytechnic. Action and research proceed under the guidance of a local authority project committee, and the programme takes account of the expressed needs of the community.

Developments already in progress include bringing residents and locally elected representatives together to discuss local problems; establishment of information and advice centres facilitating two-way communication between residents and local government officers and representatives of central Government departments; schemes for the benefit of children and young people; and the provision of recreational facilities and environmental improvements. Studies now under way, or beginning, are into such things as the means of advancing educational opportunities in areas of high social need (community schools programmes), new approaches in adult education, patterns of employment and mobility, housing and development policies, and the co-ordination of the work of the new social services departments of local authorities with that of other service departments having a common interest in the meeting of social needs.

STAFFING THE SOCIAL SERVICES

THERE ARE two broad classes of people engaged full time in the social services. On the one hand there are the specialists technically qualified for a particular profession or occupation, for example, teachers, doctors or qualified social workers. On the other there are those employed by public authorities or voluntary bodies to administer the social services; these include people with specialised functions such as disablement resettlement officers or youth employment officers, who receive some in-service training for this work, as well as organisers and office workers. In addition, there are the voluntary workers who work unpaid in the social services in their own spare time, in particular by giving personal service, for example, as youth leaders, visitors to old people, marriage guidance counsellors or members of the Women's Royal Voluntary Service.

TEACHERS

School teachers are appointed by the local education authorities or, in the case of independent or voluntary schools, by the governors or managers of the school. Teachers in maintained schools must hold qualifications approved by the education departments. The majority of teachers in England and Wales qualify by taking a three-year course at a college of education (see p 59). Increasing numbers of students obtain a degree and a professional qualification by taking a four-year Bachelor of Education course. For graduates and people with certain other specialist qualifications an additional year's compulsory professional training is gradually being introduced.

The Government announced in December 1972 its acceptance of the main recommendations made by the committee of inquiry into Teacher Education and Training (see Reading List, p 116). These proposals are designed to improve the standard of teaching through an expansion of the system of induction and in-service training. Educational studies are also to be revised with the ultimate objective of an all-graduate profession. A three-year B.Ed course is proposed which will lead to qualified status and the possibility of continuing for a fourth year to take an Honours B.Ed degree.

In Scotland teachers in secondary schools must be graduates, or the equivalent, and must have taken a course of teacher training but primary school teachers may qualify by taking a three-year course at a college of education. The General Teaching Council in Scotland has almost complete power over the profession, excluding salary matters, and maintains a register of qualified teachers. Proposals for establishing a similar body for England and Wales are under consideration. There are national salary scales for teachers in schools and other educational institutions maintained from public funds.

THE MEDICAL, DENTAL, NURSING AND ALLIED PROFESSIONS

Only people whose names are on the medical and dental registers respectively may practise as doctors and dentists under the National Health Service.

Dental auxiliaries (who have undergone a two-year training course) may carry out some kinds of simple dental work under the direction of a registered dentist. The minimum qualification for registration as a doctor requires five to seven years' training in medical school and hospital, with an additional year's experience as a resident assistant doctor in a hospital; for a dentist, four or more years at a dental school are required. The governing body of the medical profession is the General Medical Council, first set up in 1858; that of the dentists is the General Dental Council which succeeded the Dental Board in 1956. The British Medical Association is the doctors' main professional association; that of the dentists is the British Dental Association.

The minimum period of hospital training required to qualify for registration as a nurse is normally three years.[1] Training may be in general, sick children's, mental or mentally subnormal nursing. An enrolled nurse takes a two-year course. The examining bodies of the nursing profession in England and Wales and in Scotland are the General Nursing Councils, and in Northern Ireland the Council for Nurses and Midwives. Midwives in England and Wales and in Scotland must have the certificate of the appropriate Central Midwives Board, and in Northern Ireland of the Council for Nurses and Midwives. Most pupil midwives are already registered general nurses or sick children's nurses; for them the two-year midwifery training period is reduced to one year and, for other registered and enrolled nurses, to 18 months. The Royal College of Nursing and the Royal College of Midwives are the professional bodies for nurses and midwives. Health visitors (see p 30) are registered general nurses who have undergone at least the first part of the midwifery course or obstetric nursing before taking a year's course in health visiting, promoted by the Council for the Education and Training of Health Visitors.

To practise as a retail or hospital pharmacist, a pharmaceutical chemist must have his or her name entered in the register maintained by the Pharmaceutical Society of Great Britain, the governing body of the profession, or by the Pharmaceutical Society of Northern Ireland. Four or five years' academic study and practical training are necessary for registration. The dispensing of all medicines and the sale of certain specified medicines can be carried out only by, or under the supervision of, a registered pharmaceutical chemist. Under the Opticians Act 1958 the General Optical Council regulates the professions of ophthalmic optician and dispensing optician; only registered ophthalmic opticians (or registered medical practitioners) may test sight. Training of ophthalmic opticians takes four years including a year of practical experience under supervision. Dispensing opticians may take a two-year full-time course with a year's practical experience or a part-time day-release course while employed with an optician.

State registration may be obtained by chiropodists, dietitians, medical laboratory technicians, occupational therapists, orthoptists, physiotherapists, radiographers and remedial gymnasts. The governing bodies are eight boards (called, for example, the Chiropodists' Board or the Dietitians' Board) under the general supervision of the Council for Professions Supplementary to

---

[1] Recommendations for changes in the nursing profession made in the report of the Committee on Nursing (see Reading List, p 118) are under consideration by the Government. The main proposals include a reduction in the age of entry from 18 to 17 and a common basic training for all nurses and midwives with opportunities for subsequent specialisation.

Medicine. A professional training lasting two to four years is needed to qualify for registration. Only members of these professions who are state registered may be employed in the National Health Service and some other public services.

Employment in the National Health Service

Some 840,000 people in Great Britain, including nearly all those engaged in the provision of medical services (see p 25), work in the National Health Service. The exceptions are that small number of practitioners who treat only private patients. Any fully registered medical or dental practitioner may take part in the National Health Service as a general practitioner and, in addition to giving medical services under the health services, he may take private patients if he wishes.

A general medical or dental practitioner is an 'independent contractor' in contract with an executive council (see p 23). The practitioner's side of the contract consists in adhering to certain statutory terms of service which lay down whom he must treat and in what circumstances, and which stipulate various obligations which he must fulfil in the course of such treatment. Executive councils are thus responsible for ensuring that the practitioner adheres to his terms of service, and will investigate any complaint which gives grounds for supposing that he may be in breach of those terms.

General practitioners are paid according to a system of fees and allowances, the level of which are based upon recommendations made by the Review Body on Doctors' and Dentists' Remuneration. Dentists who provide treatment under the general dental services are paid a fee for each item of treatment given. The Review Body also makes recommendations on the pay of ophthalmic medical practitioners (ophthalmic opticians and dispensing opticians have their pay negotiated through the appropriate Whitley Council).

Hospital staffs are not employed by the Department of Health and Social Security but are officers of the Regional Hospital Boards or Boards of Governors of teaching hospitals. In the case of Regional Hospital Boards the responsibility for appointing and dismissing the majority of staff has been delegated to Hospital Management Committees. The scales of remuneration of consultants and other doctors and dentists in the hospital service are also based on the recommendations of the Review Body on Doctors' and Dentists' Remuneration.

The pay of other health service employees is determined by the Secretary of State in the light of negotiations between the management and staff sides of the health service Whitley Councils—joint negotiating bodies which cover the majority of health service employees. The national Whitley machine consists of a General Council which deals with matters of general interest, and nine functional councils which deal with the remuneration and conditions of service of the staff within their group, for example, nursing and midwifery, administrative and clerical, professional and technical, and ancillary staff.

In addition to fully qualified medical staff there is an increasing number of ancillary staff, such as catering and laundry staff, and porters. In 1971 there were 238,000 ancillary workers in Great Britain.

SOCIAL WORKERS

Social workers are employed in the local authority services, hospital social work departments, the probation and after-care service and in voluntary agencies. Recently a number of changes have taken place in the organisation of the social services in Britain which are reflected in current social work training developments. The most important change came as a result of the Local Authority Social Services Act 1970 (see p 34) which required local authorities in England and Wales to establish new unified social services departments to take over and integrate most of the child care and welfare functions and certain of the health services previously administered by separate local authority departments. Similar integration has taken place in Scotland under the Social Work (Scotland) Act 1968 (see p 34). This re-organisation has caused social work training to become less specialist and more 'generic' in its approach.

To help rationalise social work training the Central Council for Education and Training in Social Work was established in 1971 to replace the Council for Training in Social Work, the Central Training Council in Child Care and the Recruitment and Training Committee of the Advisory Council for Probation and After-Care. The new council is responsible for promoting and recognising professional training in all fields of social work throughout Britain. Students who satisfactorily complete recognised qualifying courses may apply to the council for the Certificate of Qualification in Social Work. This certificate may be gained by both graduates and non-graduates. Graduates with a non-relevant degree can do a two-year postgraduate course, probably at a university, while graduates with a relevant degree such as sociology with social administration involving practical experience of social work need only do a one-year course. Non-graduates may apply to a number of colleges of further education and polytechnics to do a two-year non-graduate course.

Other qualifications awarded by the Central Council include certificates for residential social work, for residential care of children and young people, and for social work with the deaf and the blind.

In June 1970 the British Association of Social Workers was formed to represent the views and interests of social workers to the Government, local authorities and voluntary agencies of all kinds. The association also has representatives on statutory advisory councils and on the governing bodies of many social work organisations. It plays an important role in raising professional standards in social work and in the negotiation of salaries and conditions of service.

Training for Voluntary Work

An important development in recent years has been the introduction of training schemes for voluntary workers. The British Red Cross Society, for example, has trained its voluntary workers for many years; the National Marriage Guidance Council carries out a rigorous method of selection and training; Citizens' Advice Bureaux workers are also carefully selected and trained.

In the Women's Royal Voluntary Service training is given for tasks of special responsibility and Age Concern arranges training courses at local, regional and national levels. An increasing number of local councils of social service provide general and introductory courses for volunteers, often in co-operation with university extra-mural boards and other adult education authorities.

THE CIVIL SERVICE[1]

Civil servants staff central departments concerned with social services whose responsibility is to administer legislation passed by Parliament. Their functions range from formulating policy proposals and the management of the machinery of government to carrying out day-to-day duties of public administration. They also staff offices at the local level, for example, the offices of the Department of Health and Social Security and employment exchanges. Full-time prison staff of all ranks, except chaplains, are also civil servants. There are nearly 700,000 civil servants, one-third of them women.

Appointment to the Home Civil Service of the British Government is the responsibility of the Civil Service Commission which is part of the Civil Service Department. As a result of the proposals of the Fulton Committee[2] an important programme of reconstruction and reform in the Civil Service was started, designed to create a classless, uniformly graded structure covering all civil servants in the 'non-industrial' part of the service.

At the top levels of the Civil Service, where staff are predominantly concerned with higher management and policy, there is now an open and unified structure, with three grades—permanent secretary, deputy secretary and under secretary—available for all types of post. Posts at these levels are filled by the people most suitable for them without regard to their academic background or to whether they were previously in a specialist or generalist stream.

At other levels it is proposed that the structure should be based on a system of categories and occupational groups. Occupational groups cater for groups of staff whose members have common personnel management and recruitment needs. Categories are pay and grading structures, each containing occupational groups. Three new categories have so far been created, and the groups of staff that are so far members of them are shown below.

General Category

The Administration Group contains some 216,000 staff. Their functions range from the co-ordination and improvement of Government machinery and the formulation of advice to ministers on matters of policy to the performance of normal clerical duties connected with the running of departmental business.

The Economist Group contains about 200 staff. They provide economic advice and undertake economic analysis.

The Statistician Group (some 350 staff) undertakes the collection and analysis of statistics required for Government policies.

The Information Officer Group (some 1,300 staff) carries out a variety of specialised press, publicity, public relations and information work.

---

[1]For fuller information, see COI reference pamphlet *The British Civil Service*, R5599.
[2]The committee appointed by the Government in 1966 under the chairmanship of Lord Fulton, then Vice-Chancellor of the University of Sussex, to examine the structure, recruitment and management, including management training, of the Civil Service which published its report on the Civil Service in June 1968.

Science Category

This contains the Science Group (16,000 staff), which is responsible for conducting scientific research and testing in numerous Government laboratories and testing establishments, and for providing advice on scientific policy. Its members also participate in the planning and management of advanced technology procurement projects.

Professional and Technical Category

This contains some 4,000 staff and includes a range of professionals—architects, engineers, doctors, nurses, and social workers—whose main function is to plan and oversee a wide range of Government construction and procurement activities, and to carry out certain inspection and regulatory activities.

Future Proposals

The three categories already established account for over half the staff in the non-industrial Civil Service, and it is proposed that the remainder should in due course be restructured by assimilation to either one or the other of these categories or by incorporation into additional categories to be set up for the purpose. Such staff include those in a number of 'general service' classes (that is to say, classes whose members serve in a number of departments) for instance the medical class (doctors advising on the planning and management of the National Health Service, running the prison medical service and undertaking duties of a similar nature), and the legal class (whose members provide legal advice and services for all Government departments).

Typists

The Civil Service employs about 25,000 shorthand typists, audio typists, and copy typists, who work mainly in small groups, and about 3,700 personal secretaries who work mainly to senior civil servants.

Other Support Staff

There are about 25,000 other support staff, including paperkeepers, office cleaners and messengers.

Northern Ireland has its own Civil Service which deals with matters transferred to its jurisdiction. Subject to regional differences, this is modelled on its counterpart in Great Britain.

In general, the civil servant receives a salary which is based on a fair comparison with that paid for similar work outside the service and usually he receives annual increments up to the maximum of the scale of the grade to which he belongs.

LOCAL GOVERNMENT SERVICE[1]

Over 2 million people are employed in local goverment service in Britain many of whom, such as teachers (see p 98), are directly concerned with providing social services. Certain appointments, for instance, the medical

---

[1]For fuller information, see COI reference pamphlet *Local Government in Britain*, R5505.

officer of health and the director of social services, are compulsory to all the authorities concerned and it has been provided that each London borough and the City of London must have a borough (or city) architect. Apart from such designated appointments, councils are normally free to employ whatever staff they consider necessary. Choice of personnel is left, to a great extent, to the individual council; a few appointments of chief officers are subject to central confirmation, but the choice of the council is nearly always accepted.

Employees are of three kinds: heads of departments whose duties are mainly of an administrative and managerial kind; a variety of officers employed in a professional, technical or clerical capacity; and a large number of manual workers who are employed to do the actual physical work for which the council may be responsible. Senior staff appointments are usually made at the instance of the committees particularly concerned, while most junior appointments are normally made by heads of departments, who are also responsible for engaging manual workers.

There is no single local government service on a national basis but movement of officers between one council and another frequently occurs. An officer in local government service may apply for a higher position under any local authority in the country. This freedom of movement is welcomed by employing councils no less than by the officers themselves, for it gives councils a wide choice in making their appointments, and means that fresh minds may be brought to a council's business.

Rates of pay and conditions of service for local authority staff are within the jurisdiction of the employing council, except in the rare cases where the proposed salary of an officer requires ministerial approval. Special arrangements are made for the staff of the GLC, while in parish councils pay and conditions are solely a matter of agreement between council and employee; elsewhere they are governed by recommendations of national joint councils consisting of representatives of the employers' side appointed by the local authority associations and representatives of the employees' side appointed by the trade unions and other officers' associations.

In view of the reorganisation of local government (see p 9) the Government has set up Staff Commissions to advise on the arrangements for transfer and recruitment of staff and for the safeguarding of staff interests.

APPENDIX

SOCIAL SERVICE DEPARTMENTS AND ORGANISATIONS
SOCIAL SECURITY

Government Departments

Department of Health and Social Security, Alexander Fleming House, London SE1 6BY.

Department of Health and Social Services, Dundonald House, Upper Newtownards Road, Belfast BT4 3SF.

Other Bodies

Royal British Legion, 49 Pall Mall, London SW1Y 5JY.

HEALTH AND PERSONAL SOCIAL SERVICES

Government Departments and Official Bodies

Department of Health and Social Security, Alexander Fleming House, Elephant and Castle, London SE1 6BY.

Scottish Home and Health Department, St Andrew's House, Edinburgh EH1 3DE.

Social Work Services Group, York Buildings, Queen Street, Edinburgh EH2 1HY.

Department of Health and Social Services, Dundonald House, Upper Newtownards Road, Belfast BT4 3SF.

Welsh Office, 42 Park Place, Cardiff CF1 3PY.

General Dental Council, 37 Wimpole Street, London W1M 8DQ.

General Medical Council, 44 Hallam Street, London W1N 6AE.

General Nursing Council for England and Wales, 23 Portland Place, London W1A 1BA.

General Optical Council, 41 Harley Street, London W1N 2DJ.

Health Education Council, Middlesex House, 1 Ealing Road, Alperton, Middlesex HA0 1HH.

Office of Population Censuses and Surveys, Somerset House, Strand, London WC2R 1LR.

Scottish Council for Health Education, 16 York Place, Edinburgh EH1 3EY.

Registrar-General for Scotland, New Register House, Edinburgh EH1 3YY.

Medical Research Council, 20 Park Crescent, London W1N 4AL.

Community Relations Commission, 15–16 Bedford Street, London WC2E 9HX.

Other Bodies

British Council for Rehabilitation of the Disabled, Tavistock House (South), Tavistock Square, London WC1H 9LB.

British Diabetic Association, 3 Alfred Place, London WC1E 7EE.

British Epilepsy Association, 3 Alfred Place, London WC1E 7ED.

British Polio Fellowship, Clifton House, Euston Road, London NW1 2RJ.

British Red Cross Society, 9 Grosvenor Crescent, London SW1X 7EJ.

British Rheumatism and Arthritis Association, 1 Devonshire Place, London W1N 2BD.

Central Council for the Disabled, 34 Eccleston Square, London SW1V 1PE.

Chest and Heart Association, Tavistock House North, Tavistock Square, London WC1H 9JE.

Invalid Children's Aid Association Incorporated, 126 Buckingham Palace Road, London SW1W 9SB.

King Edward's Hospital Fund for London, 14 Palace Court, London W2 4HT.
Mental After-Care Association, 110 Jermyn Street, London SW1Y 6HD.
National Association for Maternal and Child Welfare, Tavistock House, Tavistock Square, London WC1H 9JG.
National Association for Mental Health, 39 Queen Anne Street, London W1M 0AJ.
National Association of Leagues of Hospital Friends, 44 Fulham Road, London SW3 6HH.
National Corporation for the Care of Old People, Nuffield Lodge, Regent's Park, London NW1 4RS.
Age Concern (National Old People's Welfare Council), 55 Gower Street, London WC1E 6HJ.
National Society for Mentally Handicapped Children, 86 Newman Street, London W1P 4AR.
Nuffield Provincial Hospitals Trust, 3 Prince Albert Road, London NW1 7SP.
Royal National Institute for the Blind, 224 Great Portland Street, London W1N 6AA.
Royal National Institute for the Deaf, 105 Gower Street, London WC1E 6AH.
Royal Society of Health, 90 Buckingham Palace Road, London SW1W 0SX.
St Dunstan's (for service war-blinded), 191 Old Marylebone Road, London NW1 5QN.
St John Ambulance Association and Brigade, 1 Grosvenor Crescent, London SW1X 7EF.
Scottish Regional Association for the Deaf, 158 West Regent Street, Glasgow G2 4RJ.
Scottish Association for Mental Health, 57 Melville Street, Edinburgh EH3 7HL.
Scottish Council for the Care of Spastics, Rhuemore, 22 Corstorphine Road, Edinburgh EH12 6HP.
Scottish Epilepsy Association, 24 St Vincent Place, Glasgow G1 2EU.
Scottish Old People's Welfare Committee, 10 Alva Street, Edinburgh EH2 4QH.
Shaftesbury Society, 112 Regency Street, London SW1P 4AP.
The Spastics Society, 12 Park Crescent, London W1N 4EQ.

SERVICES FOR FAMILIES

Government Departments

Department of Health and Social Security, Alexander Fleming House, Elephant and Castle, London SE1 6BY.
Department of Home Affairs, Dundonald House, Upper Newtownards Road, Belfast BT4 3SF.
Scottish Education Department, St Andrew's House, Edinburgh EH1 3DB.
Scottish Home and Health Department, St Andrew's House, Edinburgh EH1 3DE.

Other Bodies

Association of British Adoption Agencies, 27 Queen Anne's Gate, London SW1H 9BU.
Catholic Marriage Advisory Council, 15 Lansdowne Road, London W11 3AJ.
Church Army, 185 Marylebone Road, London NW1 5QL.
Church of England Committee for Social Work and the Social Services, Church House, Dean's Yard, London SW1P 3PA.
Church of Scotland Committee on Social Service, 121 George Street, Edinburgh EH2 4YN.
Dr Barnardo's, Tanners Lane, Barkingside, Ilford, Essex.
Family Planning Association, Margaret Pyke House, 27–35 Mortimer Street, London W1A 4QW.
Family Service Units, 207 Old Marylebone Road, London NW1 5QP.

Family Welfare Association, Denison House, 296 Vauxhall Bridge Road, London SW1V 1AP.

National Adoption Society, 47A Manchester Street, London W1M 6DJ.

National Children's Bureau, 1 Fitzroy Square, London W1P 5AH.

National Council for One-Parent Families, 255 Kentish Town Road, London NW5 2LX.

National Council of Voluntary Child Care Organisations, 85 Highbury Park, London N5 1UD.

National Marriage Guidance Council, 58 Queen Anne Street, London W1M 0BT.

NSPCC (National Society for the Prevention of Cruelty to Children), 1 Riding House Street, London W1P 7PA.

Scottish Council for the Unmarried Mother and Her Child, 44 Albany Street, Edinburgh EH1 3QR.

Scottish Marriage Guidance Council, 45 Manor Place, Edinburgh EH3 7EB.

Shelter, 86 Strand, London WC2R 0EQ.

EDUCATION

Government Departments and Official Bodies

Department of Education and Science, Elizabeth House, York Road, London SE1 7PH.

Welsh Education Office, 31 Cathedral Road, Cardiff CF1 9UJ.

Scottish Education Department, St Andrew's House, Edinburgh EH1 3DB.

Department of Education (Northern Ireland), Rathgael House, Balloo Road, Bangor, County Down.

British Council, 65 Davies Street, London W1Y 2AA.

Council for National Academic Awards, 3 Devonshire Street, London W1N 2BA.

University Grants Committee, 14 Park Crescent, London W1N 4DH.

Other Bodies

Advisory Centre for Education (ACE), 57 Russell Street, Cambridge CB2 1HU.

Association of Commonwealth Universities, 36 Gordon Square, London WC1H 0PF.

British Association for Commercial and Industrial Education (BACIE), 16 Park Crescent, London W1N 4AP.

Catholic Educational Council, 41 Cromwell Road, London SW7 2DJ.

Central Bureau for Educational Visits and Exchanges, 91 Victoria Street, London SW1H 0HU.

Educational Interchange Council, 43 Russell Square, London WC1B 5DG.

National Committee for Audio-Visual Aids in Education, 33 Queen Anne Street, London W1M 0AL.

National Council for Diplomas in Art and Design, 16 Park Crescent, London W1N 4DN.

National Federation of Women's Institutes, 39 Eccleston Street, London SW1W 9NT.

National Foundation for Educational Research in England and Wales, The Mere, Upton Park, Slough, Bucks SL1 2DQ.

National Institute of Adult Education, 35 Queen Anne Street, London W1M 0BL.

National Union of Teachers, Hamilton House, Mabledon Place, London WC1H 9BB.

Nursery School Association of Great Britain and Northern Ireland, 89 Stamford Street, London SE1 9ND.

Pre-School Playgroups Association, Alford House, Aveline Street, London SE11 5DJ.

Priority Area Children, 32 Trumpington Street, Cambridge CB2 1QY.

Schools Council, 160 Great Portland Street, London W1N 6LL.
Scottish Council for Research in Education, 46 Moray Place, Edinburgh EH3 6BQ.
Universities Central Council on Admissions, PO Box 28, Cheltenham, Gloucestershire GL50 1HY.

YOUTH SERVICE

Government Departments—*As under Education*

Other Bodies

Central Council of Physical Recreation, 26 Park Crescent, London W1N 4AJ.
Church of England Youth Council, Church House, Dean's Yard, London SW1P 3NZ.
Duke of Edinburgh's Award, 2 Old Queen Street, London SW1H 9HR.
'Enterprise Youth', 29 Queen Street, Edinburgh EH2 1JX.
King George's Jubilee Trust, 166 Piccadilly, London W1V 9DE.
National Association of Youth Clubs, 30 Devonshire Street, London W1N 2AP.
National Council for Voluntary Youth Services, 26 Bedford Square, London WC1B 3HU.
National Playing Fields Association, 57B Catherine Place, London SW1E 6EY.
Outward Bound Trust, Iddesleigh House, Caxton Street, London SW1H 0PU.
Scottish Council of Physical Recreation, 4 Queensferry Street, Edinburgh EH2 4PB.
Scottish Standing Conference of Voluntary Youth Organisations, 8 Palmerston Place, Edinburgh EH12 5AA.
Scottish Youth Hostels Association, 161 Warrender Park Road, Edinburgh EH9 1EQ.
Young Volunteer Force Foundation, Abbey House, 2–8 Victoria Street, London SW1H 0LB.
Youth Hostels Association, Trevelyan House, St Stephen's Hill, St Albans, Hertfordshire.
Youth Service Information Centre, Humberstone Drive, Leicester LE5 0RG.

HOUSING

Government Departments and Official Bodies

Department of the Environment, 2 Marsham Street, London SW1P 3EB.
Scottish Development Department, St Andrew's House, Edinburgh EH1 3DD.
Department of Development, Stormont, Belfast BT4 3SS.
Housing Corporation, Sloane Square House, London SW1W 8NT.
Scottish Special Housing Association, 15 Palmerston Place, Edinburgh EH12 5AJ.
Northern Ireland Housing Executive, College Square East, Belfast BT1 6BQ.

Other Bodies

The Housing Centre Trust, 13 Suffolk Street, London SW1Y 4HG.
National Federation of Housing Societies, 86 Strand, London WC2R 0EG.

EMPLOYMENT

Government Departments and Official Bodies

Department of Employment, 8 St James's Square, London SW1Y 4JB.
Department of Health and Social Services, Dundonald House, Upper Newtownards Road, Belfast BT4 3SB.
Remploy Ltd, 415 Edgware Road, London NW2 6LR.

Other Bodies

Confederation of British Industry, 21 Tothill Street, London SW1H 9LP.

British Institute of Management, Management House, Parker Street, London WC2B 5PT.
Industrial Society, 48 Bryanston Square, London W1H 8AH.
Trades Union Congress, Great Russell Street, London WC1B 3LS.

LEGAL AID AND ADVICE
Government Department
Lord Chancellor's Office, House of Lords, London SW1A 0PW.

Other Bodies
The Law Society, 113 Chancery Lane, London WC2A 1PL.
Law Society of Scotland, 26–27 Drumsheugh Gardens, Edinburgh EH3 7YR.
The Incorporated Law Society of Northern Ireland, Legal Aid Department, Royal Courts of Justice, Chichester Street, Belfast BT1 3JZ.

TREATMENT OF OFFENDERS
Government Departments and Official Bodies
Home Office, Whitehall, London SW1A 2AP.
Scottish Home and Health Department, St Andrew's House, Edinburgh EH1 3DE.
Department of Home Affairs, Dundonald House, Upper Newtownards Road, Belfast BT4 3SU.

Other Bodies
Howard League for Penal Reform, 125 Kennington Park Road, London SE11 4JP.
National Association for the Care and Resettlement of Offenders, 125 Kennington Park Road, London SE11 4JP.

VOLUNTARY ORGANISATIONS[1]
Charity Commission, 14 Ryder Street, London SW1Y 6AH.
Citizens' Advice Bureaux, 26 Bedford Square, London WC1B 3HU.
Disabled Living Foundation, 346 Kensington High Street, London W14 8NS.
Jewish Welfare Board, 74A Charlotte Street, London W1P 2AH.
National Association of Voluntary Hostels, 33 Long Acre, London WC2E 9LA.
National Council for Civil Liberties, 152 Camden High Street, London NW1 0NN.
National Council of Social Service, 26 Bedford Square, London WC1B 3HU.
Nuffield Foundation, Nuffield Lodge, Regent's Park, London NW1 4RS.
Salvation Army, 101 Queen Victoria Street, London EC4P 4EP.
Scottish Council of Social Service, 18/19 Claremont Crescent, Edinburgh EH7 4QD.
Society of Friends, Friends House, Euston Road, London NW1 2BJ.
Soldiers', Sailors' and Airmen's Families' Association, 114 Draycott Avenue, London SW3 3AF.
Volunteer Centre, 24 Nutford Place, London W1H 5YN.
Women's Royal Voluntary Service, 17 Old Park Lane, London W1V 4AJ.

STAFFING
Government Departments and Official Bodies
Advisory Council for Probation and After-Care, Romney House, Marsham Street, London SW1P 3DY.
Central Council for Education and Training in Social Work, Clifton House, Euston Road, London NW1 2RS.

---

[1]That is, charitable trusts and social agencies not listed above.

Civil Service Department, Civil Service Commission, Alencon Link, Basingstoke, Hants RG21 1JB.

Council for the Training of Health Visitors, Clifton House, Euston Road, London NW1 2RR.

Northern Ireland Civil Service Commission, Claredon House, Adelaide Street, Belfast BT2 8ND.

Other Bodies

Assistant Masters Association, 29 Gordon Square, London WC1H 0PP.

Association of Assistant Mistresses in Secondary Schools, 29 Gordon Square, London WC1H 0PP.

Association of Public Health Inspectors, 19 Grosvenor Place, London SW1X 7HP.

Association of Teachers in Colleges and Departments of Education, 151 Gower Street, London WC1E 6BA.

Association of Teachers in Technical Institutions, Hamilton House, Mabledon Place, London WC1H 9BB.

Association of University Teachers, Bremar House, Sale Place, London W2 1PS.

British Association of Social Workers, 16 Kent Street, Birmingham.

British Medical Association, BMA House, Tavistock Square, London WC1H 9JP.

Federation of Associations of Mental Health Workers, 43 Queen Anne Street, London W1M 9FA.

Headmasters' Conference, 29 Gordon Square, London WC1H 0PP.

Health Visitors' Association, 36 Eccleston Square, London SW1V 1PF.

Institute of Housing Managers, Victoria House, Southampton Row, London WC1B 4EB.

Joint University Council for Social and Public Administration, 218 Sussex Gardens, London W2 3UD.

National Association of Prison Visitors, 47 Hartington Street, Bedford.

National Association of Probation Officers, 6 Endsleigh Street, London WC1H 0DS.

National Association of Schoolmasters, Swan Court, Waterhouse Street, Hemel Hempstead.

National Institute for Social Work Training, 5 Tavistock Place, London WC1H 9SS.

National Union of Teachers, Hamilton House, Mabledon Place, London WC1H 9BB.

Queen's Institute of District Nursing, 57 Lower Belgrave Street, London SW1W 0LR.

Royal College of General Practitioners, 14 Princes Gate, London SW7 5LD.

Royal College of Midwives, 15 Mansfield Street, London W1M 0BE.

Royal College of Nursing and National Council of Nurses of the UK, 1A Henrietta Place, London W1M 0AB.

Royal College of Obstetricians and Gynaecologists, 27 Sussex Place, Regent's Park, London NW1 4RG.

Royal College of Physicians, 11 St Andrew's Place, London NW1 4LE.

Royal College of Physicians, 9 Queen Street, Edinburgh EH2 1JQ.

Royal College of Surgeons of Edinburgh, 18 Nicolson Street, Edinburgh EH8 9DW.

Royal College of Surgeons of England, Lincoln's Inn Fields, London WC2A 3PN.

Royal College of Physicians and Surgeons, 242 St Vincent Street, Glasgow G2 5RJ.

Royal Institute of British Architects, 66 Portland Place, London W1N 4AD.

Royal Institute of Public Health and Hygiene, 28 Portland Place, London W1N 4DE.

Royal Society of Health, 90 Buckingham Palace Road, London SW1W 0SX.

Social Work Advisory Service, 26 Bloomsbury Way, London WC1A 2SR.

Society of Medical Officers of Health, Tavistock House (South), Tavistock Square, London WC1H 9LD.

READING LIST

General £

BROWN, M. Introduction to Social Administration in Britain.
ISBN 0 09 098800 0. *Hutchinson* 1969 1·25
FORDER, A. (*Editor.*) Penelope Hall's Social Services of England
and Wales. *ISBN 0 7100 7057 8.* *Routledge* 1971 2·25
GREGG, PAULINE. The Welfare State. *ISBN 0 245 58548 6. Harrap* 1967 2·00
HALSEY, A. H. (*Editor.*) Trends in British Society since 1900: A
Guide to the Changing Social Structure of Britain.
ISBN 0 333 10549 4. *Macmillan* 1972 4·95
MARSH, DAVID. The Welfare State.
ISBN 0 582 48769 2. *Longman* 1970 1·60
WILLMOTT, PHYLLIS. Consumer's Guide to the British Social
Services. Third edition. *ISBN 0 14 020871 2.* *Penguin* 1973 0·50
——— Public Social Services: Handbook of Information. Thir-
teenth edition. *ISBN 0 7199 0861 2.*
National Council of Social Service 1973 1·25
Guide to the Social Services 1973. Family Welfare Association.
ISBN 0 7121 0716 9. *Macdonald & Evans* 1972 0·85
The General Household Survey: Introductory Report.
SBN 11 700681 5. *HMSO* 1973 1·80
Race Relations in Britain. COI reference pamphlet.
SBN 11 700613 0. *HMSO* 1972 0·36
Social Trends No. 3, 1972. *Annual.* *HMSO*

Social Security

BOULTON, A. HARDING. Law and Practice of Social Security.
ISBN 0 85308 025 9. *Jordan & Sons* 1972 1·95
GEORGE, V. N. Social Security: Beveridge and After.
ISBN 0 7100 6205 2. *Routledge* 1968 2·10
GILBERT, B. B. The Evolution of National Insurance in Great
Britain. *ISBN 0 7181 0480 3.* *Michael Joseph* 1966 4·20
Social Insurance and Allied Services [Beveridge Report].
Cmd 6404. *HMSO* 1942 1·25
Social Security in Britain. COI reference pamphlet.
SBN 11 700619 X. *HMSO* 1973 0·36
Strategy for Pensions—The Future of State and Occupational
Pensions. Cmnd 4755. *SBN 10 147550 0.* *HMSO* 1971 0·25
Proposals for a Tax Credit System. Cmnd 5116.
SBN 10 151160 4. *HMSO* 1972 0·29

Health and Personal Social Services

BROCKINGTON, C. F. A Short History of Public Health. Second
edition. *ISBN 0 7000 1031 9.* *J. & A. Churchill* 1966 1·75
FOREN, R. *and* BROWN, M. J. Planning for Service. An Examina-
tion of the Organisation and Administration of Local Authority
Social Services Departments.
ISBN 0 85314 087 1. *Charles Knight* 1971 2·00
FORSYTH, GORDON. Doctors and State Medicine: a Study of the
British Health Service. *Pitman (Medical)* 1966 1·50

			£
JONES, KATHLEEN. A History of the Mental Health Services.			
ISBN 0 7100 7452 2.	Routledge & Kegan Paul	1972	5·00
LEE, MICHAEL. Opting out of the NHS. PEP Broadsheet 557.			
ISBN 0 85374 038 0.	Research Publications	1971	0·50
MEDAWAR, J. and PYKE, D. Family Planning.			
ISBN 0 14 021154 3.	Penguin	1971	0·35
NATIONAL SOCIETY FOR CLEAN AIR. Clean Air Year Book.			
	NSCA		
Annual Reports:			
Central Health Services Council.	HMSO		
Department of Health and Social Security.	HMSO		
On the State of the Public Health.	HMSO		
Health Education Council.	The Council		
Hospital Advisory Service.	HMSO		
Scottish Education Department. Social Work in Scotland.	HMSO		
Scottish Home and Health Department and Scottish Health Services Council. Health Services in Scotland.	HMSO		
Health and Welfare: The Development of Community Care. Revision to 1975–76. Cmnd 3022.	HMSO	1966	1·87½
Health Services in Britain. COI reference pamphlet. SBN 11 700620 3.	HMSO	1973	0·68
The Hospital Building Programme. A revision of the Hospital Plan for England and Wales. Cmnd 3000.	HMSO	1966	0·30
Second Review of the Hospital Plan for Northern Ireland 1970–75. Cmd 556. SBN 337 10556 1.	Belfast HMSO	1971	0·17½
National Health Service Reorganisation, England. Cmnd 5055. SBN 10 150550 7.	HMSO	1972	0·68
Management Arrangements for the Reorganised National Health Service. SBN 11 320480 9.	HMSO	1972	0·29
National Health Service Reorganisation in Wales. Cmnd 5057. SBN 10 150570 1.	HMSO	1972	0·26½
Rehabilitation and Care of Disabled People in Britain. Reference pamphlet, R4972.	COI	1972	0·75
The Rehabilitation of Drug Addicts. Report of the Advisory Committee on Drug Dependence. SBN 11 340078 0.	HMSO	1968	0·20
Reorganisation of the Scottish Health Services. Cmnd 4734. SBN 10 147340 0.	HMSO	1971	0·12½
Report of the Committee on Local Authority and Allied Personal Social Services [Seebohm Report]. Cmnd 3703. SBN 10 137030 X.	HMSO	1968	1·55
Report of the Royal Commission on Medical Education. Cmnd 3659. SBN 10 136590 X.	HMSO	1968	1·42½
Review of the Hospital Plan for Scotland. Cmnd 2877.	HMSO	1966	0·07½
Summary Report on 'An Integrated Service: the Reorganisation of Health and Personal Social Services in Northern Ireland'. SBN 337 07052 0.	Belfast HMSO	1972	0·31½

The Elderly

AGE CONCERN AT WORK. Annual Report of the National Old People's Welfare Council.	Age Concern		free
CONSUMERS' ASSOCIATION. Arrangements for Old Age. ISBN 0 85202 037 6.	Consumers' Association	1969	0·75

			£
NATIONAL CORPORATION FOR THE CARE OF OLD PEOPLE. Annual Report.	*NCCOP*		free
ROBERTS, NESTA. Our Future Selves: care of the elderly. *ISBN 0 04 362017 5.*	*Allen & Unwin*	1970	1·75
TOWNSEND, P. *and* WEDDERBURN, DOROTHY. The Aged in the Welfare State. *ISBN 0 7135 0956 2.*	*Bell*	1965	1·05
Care of the Elderly in Britain. Reference paper, R5850.	*COI*	1969	0·13

Children

BOSS, PETER. Exploration into Child Care. *ISBN 0 7100 6965 0.*	*Routledge*	1971	1·50
BROMLEY, P. M. Family Law. *ISBN 0 406 56003 X.*	*Butterworths*	1971	6·00
JACKA, ALAN A. Adoption in Brief. *ISBN 0 85633 015 9.*	*NFER*	1973	1·30
PARFIT, J. Spotlight on Services for the Young Handicapped Child. *ISBN 0 902817 04 3.*	*National Children's Bureau*	1972	1·50
PRINGLE, M. L. KELLMER. Adoption—Facts and Fallacies. *ISBN 0 582 32422 X.*	*Longman*	1967	1·10

Annual Reports:

Children in Care in England and Wales.	*HMSO*		
Children's Department of the Home Office. Report on Work.	*HMSO*		
Report on the Administration of Home Office Services.	*Belfast HMSO*		
Children in Britain. COI reference pamphlet. *SBN 11 700618 1.*	*HMSO*	1973	0·47
A Guide to Adoption Practice. Advisory Council on Child Care. *SBN 11 340356 9.*	*HMSO*	1970	0·75
Report of the Departmental Committee on the Adoption of Children. Cmnd 5107. *SBN 10 151070 5.*	*HMSO*	1972	0·90
Home Office. Part 1 of the Children and Young Persons Act 1969: a guide for courts and practitioners. *SBN 11 340335 6.*	*HMSO*	1970	0·32½

Education

ARGLES, MICHAEL. South Kensington to Robbins: An Account of Technical and Scientific Education since 1851. *ISBN 0 582 32383 5.*	*Longman*	1964	1·25
ASSOCIATION OF COMMONWEALTH UNIVERSITIES. Commonwealth Universities Yearbook.	*The Association*		
—— Awards for Commonwealth University Staff.	*The Association*		
ASSOCIATION OF TEACHERS IN COLLEGES AND DEPARTMENTS OF EDUCATION. Handbook for Colleges and Departments of Education.	*Lund Humphries*		
BARON, GEORGE. A Bibliographical Guide to the English Educational System. Third edition. *ISBN 0 485 11078 4.*	*Athlone Press*	1965	0·90
BENN, C. *and* SIMON, B. Halfway There (Comprehensive Schools). *ISBN 0 14 080697 0.*	*Penguin*	1972	1·50
BOYLE, EDWARD *and* CROSLAND, ANTHONY. The Politics of Education. *ISBN 0 14 080607 5.*	*Penguin*	1971	0·35

		£
BRITISH COUNCIL. Annual Report. *British Council*

BRITISH COUNCIL *and* THE ASSOCIATION OF COMMONWEALTH UNIVERSITIES. Higher Education in the United Kingdom: A Handbook for Students from Overseas. *Biennial. Longman*

BURGESS, TYRRELL. A Guide to English Schools.
ISBN 0 14 020690 6. *Penguin* 1972 0·35

—— *and* PRATT, JOHN. Policy and Practice: The Colleges of Advanced Technology. *ISBN 0 7139 0151 9.* *Allen Lane* 1970 5·25

COMMITTEE OF VICE-CHANCELLORS AND PRINCIPALS OF THE UNIVERSITIES OF THE UNITED KINGDOM. A Compendium of Entrance Requirements for First Degree Courses in the United Kingdom. *Annual.* *The Committee*

COUNCIL FOR NATIONAL ACADEMIC AWARDS. Compendium of Degree Courses. *CNAA* free

—— Report. *CNAA* free

DENT, H. C. The Educational System of England and Wales.
ISBN 0 340 15465 9. *University of London Press* 1971 1·00

Education Committees Year Book. *Councils and Education Press*

FINDLAY, IAN R. Education in Scotland.
ISBN 0 7153 5744 1. *David and Charles* 1973 2·75

HALSEY, A. H. *and* TROW, MARTIN. The British Academics.
ISBN 0 571 09585 2. *Faber* 1971 5·00

HUNTER, S. LESLIE. The Scottish Educational System.
ISBN 0 08 016668 7. *Pergamon* 1972 1·65

JACKSON, STEPHEN. Special Education in England and Wales.
ISBN 0 19 919001 1. *Oxford University Press* 1969 0·75

KELLY, THOMAS. A History of Adult Education.
ISBN 0 85323 230 X. *Liverpool University Press* 1970 3·25

LOMAX, D. E. (*Editor.*) The Education of Teachers in Britain.
ISBN 0 471 54380 2. *John Wiley and Sons* 1973 5·50

MACLURE, J. STUART. Educational Documents, England and Wales, 1816–1968. *ISBN 0 416 41830 9.* *Chapman & Hall* 1968 1·25

NATIONAL INSTITUTE OF ADULT EDUCATION. Adult Education in the United Kingdom. A Directory of Organisations. *Annual.*
National Institute of Adult Education

OPEN UNIVERSITY. The Early Development of the Open University: Report of the Vice-Chancellor Jan. 1969–Dec. 1970.
The University

—— The First Teaching Year of the Open University. Report of the Vice-Chancellor 1971. *The University*

PEERS, R. Adult Education: A Comparative Study.
ISBN 0 7100 7410 7. *Routledge & Kegan Paul* 1973 6·50

Provision for Adult Education.
ISBN 0 900559 04 7. *National Institute of Adult Education* 1970 2·10

PERKIN, H. J. New Universities in the United Kingdom. *OECD* 1969 2·40

ROBINSON, ERIC E. The New Polytechnics.
ISBN 0 14 080041 7. *Penguin* 1968 0·30

UNIVERSITIES CENTRAL COUNCIL ON ADMISSIONS. *Annual. UCCA*

WARDLE, D. English Popular Education 1780–1970.
ISBN 0 521 09631 6. *Cambridge University Press* 1970 0·60

Annual Reports:
Department of Education and Science (England and Wales): Education Statistics for the United Kingdom. *HMSO*

Education and Science. *HMSO*
Statistics of Education (6 volumes):
    Vol 1: Schools. *HMSO*
    Vol 2: School Leavers, GCE and CSE. *HMSO*
    Vol 3: Further Education. *HMSO*
    Vol 4: Teachers. *HMSO*
    Vol 5: Finance and Awards. *HMSO*
    Vol 6: Universities. *HMSO*
Department of Education for Northern Ireland:
    Education in Northern Ireland. *Belfast HMSO*
    Education Statistics (two series). *Belfast HMSO*
Scottish Education Department:
    Education in Scotland. *HMSO*
    Scottish Educational Statistics. *HMSO*

Adult Education: A Plan For Development [Russell Report].
SBN 11 270336 4. *HMSO* 1973 1·90

Children and their Primary Schools: Report of the Central
Advisory Council for Education (England) [Plowden Report].
    Vol 1: Report. *HMSO* 1967 1·25
    Vol 2: Research and Surveys. *HMSO* 1967 1·62½

Educational Priority—EPA Problems and Policies—Vol 1.
(Report of a research project sponsored by the Department
of Education and Science and the Social Science Research
Council.) *SBN 11 270295 3.* *HMSO* 1972 1·20

Education: A Framework for Expansion. Cmnd 5174.
SBN 10 151740 8. *HMSO* 1972 0·31½

Education in Britain. COI reference pamphlet.
SBN 11 700119 8. *HMSO* 1971 0·73

Education in Scotland: A Statement of Policy. Cmnd 5175.
SBN 10 151750 5. *HMSO* 1972 0·13½

Educational Techniques in Britain. Reference paper, R5754.
COI 1972 0·21

Educational Television and Radio in Britain. Reference paper,
R5781. *COI* 1971 0·5

The Education of Immigrants. Education Survey 13.
SBN 11 270201 5. *HMSO* 1971 0·85

The Health of the School Child. Report of the Chief Medical
Officer of the Department of Education and Science.
Biennial. *HMSO*

Inside the Colleges of Further Education (by Adrian Bristow).
SBN 11 270174 4. *HMSO* 1970 0·30

Inside Comprehensive Schools (by Tyrrell Burgess).
SBN 11 270149 3. *HMSO* 1970 0·30

Inside the Primary School (by John Blackie).
SBN 11 270048 9. *HMSO* 1967 0·25

Plan for Polytechnics and Other Colleges: Higher Education in
the Further Education System. Cmnd 3006. *HMSO* 1966 0·09

Primary Education in Wales. *HMSO* 1968 1·62½

Public Education in Scotland. Seventh edition.
SBN 11 490787 0. *HMSO* 1972 0·47

Technician Courses and Examinations. Report of the [Hasle-
grave] Committee. *SBN 11 270143 4.* *HMSO* 1969 0·62½

			£
Teacher Education and Training [James Report].			
SBN 11 270236 8.	HMSO	1972	0·85
Universities in Britain. Reference paper, R5520.	COI	1973	0·21
University Grants Committee. Annual Survey.	HMSO		

The Youth Service

Duke of Edinburgh's Award Scheme. Annual Report.			
	Duke of Edinburgh's Award Office		free
LEIGH, JOHN. Young People and Leisure.			
ISBN 0 7100 7059 4.	Routledge	1971	1·50
MILSON, FRED. Youth in a Changing Society.			
ISBN 0 7100 7204 X.	Routledge	1972	1·50
NATIONAL COUNCIL OF SOCIAL SERVICE. Youth in Action.			
ISBN 0 7199 0811 6.	NCSS	1971	0·40
Year Book of the Youth Service in England and Wales 1972–73.			
ISBN 0 902095 93 5.	Youth Service Information Centre	1973	4·00
Youth and Community Work in the 70's.			
SBN 11 270014 4.	HMSO	1969	0·75
The Youth Service and Similar Provisions for Young People.			
SBN 11 700128 7.	HMSO	1972	3·00
The Youth Service in Britain, Reference paper, R5506.	COI	1973	0·21

Housing

PAGE, DILYS *and* MUIR, TOM. New Housing for the Elderly.			
ISBN 0 7199 08183.	NCCOP	1971	0·75
Better Homes: the Next Priorities. Cmnd 5339. *SBN 10 153390 X.*			
	HMSO	1973	0·13½
Fair Deal for Housing. Cmnd 4728. *SBN 10 147280 3.*	HMSO	1971	0·22½
Homes for People: Scottish Housing Policy in the 1970s.			
Cmnd 5272. *SBN 10 152720 9.*	HMSO	1973	0·13
Homes for Today and Tomorrow [Parker Morris Report].			
	HMSO	1961	0·20
Housing Associations. *SBN 11 750370 3.*	HMSO	1971	0·80
Housing in Britain. COI reference pamphlet.			
SBN 11 700096 5.	HMSO	1970	0·27½
Housing and Construction Statistics. *Quarterly.*	HMSO		0·75
The Reform of Housing Finance in Scotland. Cmnd 4727.			
SBN 10 147270 6.	HMSO	1971	0·12½
Report of the Committee on the Rent Acts. Cmnd 4609.			
SBN 10 146090 2.	HMSO	1971	2·85
Towards Better Homes: Proposals for Dealing with Scotland's			
Older Housing. Cmnd 5338. *SBN 10 153380 2.*	HMSO	1973	0·13
Widening the Choice: the Next Steps in Housing. Cmnd 5280.			
SBN 10 152800 0.	HMSO	1973	0·13

New Towns

EVANS, HAZEL. (*Editor.*) New Towns: The British Experience.			
ISBN 0 85314 156 8.	Charles Knight	1972	4·50
OSBORN, *Sir* F. *and* WHITTICK, A. The New Towns: The Answer			
to Megalopolis. *ISBN 0 249 38983 5.*	Leonard Hill	1969	8·75
The New Towns of Britain. COI reference pamphlet.			
SBN 11 700341 7.	HMSO	1972	0·42

Employment

People and Jobs: A Modern Employment Service.
Department of Employment 1971 free
Training for the Future: A Plan for Discussion.
Department of Employment 1972 free
Into Action: Plan for a Modern Employment Service.
Department of Employment 1973 free
Year Book of Technical Education and Training for Industry.
A. & C. Black
Labour Law: Volume 1. Employment, Welfare and Safety at Work. *ISBN 0 14 080113 8.* *Penguin* 1971 0·75
Safety and Health at Work [Robens Report]. Cmnd 5034.
SBN 10 150340 7. *HMSO* 1972 1·30
Employment Medical Advisory Service Act 1972—Guide to the Service. *Department of Employment* free

Annual Reports:
Chief Inspector of Factories. *HMSO*
Chief Inspector of Mines and Quarries. *HMSO*

Legal Aid

Guide to New Legal Aid. *HMSO* 1973 free
Annual Reports:
The Law Society on the Legal Aid and Advice Act. *HMSO*
The Law Society of Scotland on the Legal Aid Scheme.
HMSO

Treatment of Offenders

MAYS, JOHN BARRON. Crime and Its Treatment.
ISBN 0 582 48113 9. *Longman* 1970 1·50
ROSE, GORDON. Schools for Young Offenders.
ISBN 0 422 70300 1. *Tavistock* 1967 2·60
WALKER, N. D. Crime and Punishment in Britain.
ISBN 0 85224 038 4. *Edinburgh University Press* 1968 1·50
WEST, D. J. The Young Offender. *ISBN 0 14 020872 0. Penguin* 1970 0·35

Annual Reports:
Criminal Injuries Compensation Board. *HMSO*
Parole Board. *HMSO*
Parole Board for Scotland. *HMSO*
Prisons in Scotland. *HMSO*
The Work of the Prison Department. *HMSO*
People in Prison. Cmnd 4214. *SBN 10 142140 0.* *HMSO* 1969 0·62½
Report on the Work of the Probation and After-Care Department, 1969–71. Cmnd 5158. *SBN 10 151580 4.* *HMSO* 1972 0·42½
The Sentence of the Court. A Handbook for Courts on the Treatment of Offenders. *HMSO* 1966 0·25
Social Work and the Community. Cmnd 3065. *HMSO* 1966 0·11
The Treatment of Offenders in Britain. COI reference pamphlet.
SBN 11 700068 X. *HMSO* 1968 0·20

Voluntary Organisations

BRASNETT, MARGARET. Voluntary Social Action: A History of the National Council of Social Services.
ISBN 0 7199 0777 2. *NCSS* 1969 1·25

			£
HOBMAN, DAVID. Who Cares? A Guide to Voluntary and Full-time Social Work. *ISBN 0 264 64556 1.* *Mowbrays*	1971	0·50
JERMAN, BETTY. Do Something: A Guide to Self Help Organisations. *ISBN 0 900391 39 1.* *Garnstone Press*	1971	1·75
MORRIS, MARY. Voluntary Work in the Welfare State. *ISBN 0 7100 6581 7.* *Routledge*	1969	2·50
NATIONAL COUNCIL OF SOCIAL SERVICE. Voluntary Social Services: Handbook of Information and Directory of Organisations. Revised edition. *NCSS*	1973	1·50
—— Directory of Grant-making Trusts. *ISBN 0 7199 0817 5.* *NCSS*	1971	5·00
Charity Commissioners for England and Wales. Annual Report. *HMSO*		

Staffing the Social Services

			£
Caring for People: Staffing Residential Homes [Williams Report]. *ISBN 0 04 360015 8.* *Allen & Unwin*	1968	1·25
TIMMS, N. Social Work. An Outline for the Intending Student. *ISBN 0 7100 6789 5.* *Routledge*	1970	1·50
The British Civil Service. Reference pamphlet, R5599. *COI*	1971	0·17
The Civil Service, Vol 1: The Report of the Committee 1966–68 [Fulton Report]. Cmnd 3638. *SBN 10 136380 X.* *HMSO*	1968	0·87½
Report of the Committee on Nursing. Cmnd 5115. *SBN 10 151150 7.* *HMSO*	1972	1·90
Staffing of Local Government. Report of the Committee. *HMSO*	1967	1·05
Teacher Training in Britain. Reference paper, R5279. *COI*	1971	0·23

Note: SBN or ISBN references should be quoted when ordering publications.

Printed in England for Her Majesty's Stationery Office by Henry Ling Ltd., Dorchester, Dorset.
Dd. 168687 K48 10/73.